BREAKTHROUGH RESULTS!

Tips, Tricks and Techniques From Today's Experts For You and Your Business

Anthology Compiled By:

WEI HOUNG

DEDICATION

This book is dedicated to all those on the team who make it possible for the rest of us to achieve breakthrough results.

While we may not say it enough, from the bottom of our hearts, we thank you for your understanding, support and love that continuously guides us on the journey to success.

TABLE OF CONTENTS

Introduction

Breakthrough Results is the second book in the Results Anthology Series. The authors in this book will provide you with the tips, tricks, and techniques to take you and your business to new heights.

With this next installment, my mission to get more business owners, entrepreneurs, corporate executives and employees, managers, financial planners, accountants, sales people, mothers, fathers, grandparents, aunts and uncles, the results they want so they can lead the life they desire continues. The authors assembled in this book were all hand-picked by me. Each represents the best in their category. Each provides outstanding information that you can use daily to achieve the results you are seeking.

When I decided to title this book "Breakthrough Results," my thought was to provide information that would allow you, the reader, to break through the obstacles you are encountering in your life and your business so you could achieve greater results, however, many of the authors in this book looked at the word breakthrough in a very different way than I did. They interpreted breakthrough results as how do you achieve the most amazing results that you could ever achieve?

This new thought was something that never even popped into my mind when I was thinking about the title. It was so unexpected. I appreciate the authors helping me to see another point of view. If you are open to learning and seeing many points of view, I believe you will be highly successful. Imagine if I hadn't had an open mind about this new interpretation. If you only take this one thought away from this book, then please walk away with a more open mind to learning. It will help you grow.

I believe we are all here to learn every day. What is so amazing for you is that as the reader you get to experience so many different points of view on a wide variety of subjects in this book. What is great about both interpretations is the fact that you, the reader, benefit both ways from our interpretations on the phrase "Breakthrough Results."

With that in mind, there are several ways to read this book. The first way is to read it cover to cover learning how to break through those obstacles to achieve the results you desire. The second way is to read it cover to cover learning how to achieve the most amazing results that you could ever achieve. The third way to read this book is to do both at the same time. The fourth way is to pick and choose the chapters that most interest you and read just those. Again, when you read those specific chapters, you may want to read that chapter either from the point of view of how to break through your obstacles or how to achieve amazing results or both.

There is a lot of amazing, helpful information in this book. Therefore, I would suggest that you highlight, bend down pages, take notes with paper and pen, or on your device to keep track of all of your learnings. There will be many nuggets that you can use. I can guarantee that!

What is also great about this book is it is here to support you in your life and your business.

So whether you read this book as a reference guide or as a motivational book or both, you will certainly learn what you need to achieve the breakthrough results you desire.

I know myself and the authors of the "Breakthrough Results" book welcome your thoughts and comments. Once you have read the book or a chapter, I urge you to reach out to that specific author that made you think or provided you with new information. Send an email to let them know your thoughts or provide some comments. I know all of us would appreciate your insights as to what moved you, changed you and got you to the results you deserve.

Thank you for letting us help you on your results-oriented journey to greater success and to an even more amazing life.

To Your RESULTS!

Jean

The Results Queen™

Chapter 1

Goodbye Goals, Hello Results

Authored by Jean Oursler

There is research that states something like less than five percent of Americans have goals and only two percent actually write their goals down. Those are pretty low numbers. I guess the theory is when you have goals and write them down you are more likely to achieve them.

How many goals have you achieved? Are you part of the five percent? Are you part of the two percent? Are you in the 95 percent group? I want you to understand that being a part of the 95 percent is not a bad thing. Just like those in the five percent group who do is a good thing. For me, there isn't any good or bad, there is just what works for you. That is the only thing that you need to keep in mind. So if goal setting and goal achieving is working for you. Stop reading and move on to the next chapter. If it isn't working for you, then read on.

Here is my question, if goals really worked, wouldn't more of us participate in having them and achieving them? With numbers like five percent or two percent, you have to wonder if this goal setting process is a hidden secret to success that many of us are just ignoring. If goals are that important to success, then what is preventing the rest of us from actually setting and achieving them?

I believe there is a host of explanations as to why more of us are not participating in setting and achieving goals. We try to set goals. We get distracted. We never get back to them. We try to set goals, and then we give up. It's too much work to set goals, so why even try. What happens when we don't achieve those goals? Won't we be a failure? Most of us don't want to be a failure, right? Why try if I am just going to fail? And the list goes on.

For many of us, we just don't see the value in goal setting. What many of us see is the negatives and pitfalls. If there is nothing positive about the goal setting experience, why would I want to participate? Unless I am forced to participate and that just makes most us want to participate in the process even less.

Here is one last exercise to really point out how negative goals can be.

Say the word "goals" out loud. How do you feel when you say that word?

Now say the word "results" out loud. How do you feel when you said that word?

Let's try it one more time. Say the word "goal" again out loud. Now say the word "result." Can you hear the difference? Can you feel the difference? When my clients do this exercise, most of them feel more positive about the word "result" than the word "goal."

Why? When you say the word "goal," normally your voice goes down. When you say the word "result," normally your voice goes up. Our brains perceive a word that goes up as more positive. Our brains perceive a word that goes down as more negative. What do you think you would respond better to – negative or positive? Most of us like the positive and will avoid the negative.

So, as long as we perceive that goals are negative, we are going to continue to ensure that we don't set goals or use goals unless we do something to make goals more positive. Most of us aren't even going down that path to make goals more positive and even if we did, most of us don't know how.

I can hear you say, "Wait a minute Jean. I never said goals were negative." Of course you didn't. That is because you are saying it on an subconscious level. Before I confuse you, let me explain.

There is the conscious level and the subconscious level. Most of us think we operate from a conscious level. The opposite is true. Most of our thoughts and behaviors happen at a subconscious level and then move to a conscious level. There are lots of times we do things that we don't know why we did them or even given much thought about. That is when you are operating from a subconscious level. Not setting goals is operating from a subconscious level. Writing goals is operating from a conscious level. So if you are in the majority of those who do not write down their goals, I just pointed out why. Now you can understand those thoughts. That is moving from the subconscious to the conscience.

So, if you have achieved every goal that you set out to achieve, then it is clear that setting goals is working for you. As I have said before, if it works for you, then keep doing it, however, if you don't even set goals, yet alone achieve every goal you set, then how well is the goal process working for you? If it doesn't work for you, then let's find the thing that does.

How do you make the goal planning process more positive? I have the answer. It is time to give up goals and get RESULTS! What do I mean by that? I think we can all agree that the goal setting process isn't working for 95 percent of us. So what will work that will help us achieve greater success? The answer is RESULTS!

How does focusing on results make us more successful? For some reason, our brains find it easier to navigate us to a result. We know the action steps we need to take. When obstacles arise, we figure out how to get around them. If it is something we truly want, we don't give up on our result. We keep working towards it no matter how long it takes. Results often happen from a subconscious level.

I believe that this behavior was honed when we were kids. Think about it. How many times do you see a kid in the store working on their parent or grandparent to get what they want? Think about when you wanted to buy a new car or a house or an Xbox? When you want a result, you are most likely unstoppable. When you have a goal, you most likely get distracted.

How do I know this? Many of my clients show up on my doorstep not having goals, yet they think they should have them. If they do have them, they are frustrated because they can't achieve them. Many of my clients are ones who have never even set a goal and wondering why they aren't more successful.

The first thing I ask my clients when we begin to work together is to give up on goals and let's focus on the results they want to achieve. When I say that, there is a switch that goes off in their heads. They can list all of the results they want. They find it easier to figure the action steps needed to get these results. If they hit an obstacle, they work themselves around it, over it or straight through it. They have had a ton of practice getting results before they ever got to my doorstep. Remember they were all kids at one time, working their parents at the toy store to get the thing they really wanted. How many kids do you see setting goals? When did you learn the goal setting process? It probably wasn't until you were older. So goal setting doesn't come as easy as results getting.

Once my clients give up on the whole goal setting process, they are more open to embracing a new way, the results way. Why?

Have you ever heard the definition of insanity? Doing the same thing over and over again expecting different results. When something isn't working for you don't keep trying hard. Get rid of it. Getting rid of it opens your mind to new things. Are you ready to get rid of the goal setting process and embrace the results way? Can I get a yes?

Please say this out loud. "I am giving up goals and I'm getting results." Say it one more time. "I am giving up goals and getting results." Doesn't that feel good? Listen to the words. Is your voice going up at the end? I bet it is. Because that is what my clients say. Remember when your voice goes up, you sound more positive and the more positive it is, the more likely we are to do it.

So now that you are about getting results. What's the process? How am I going to achieve my results? What I do when I work with my clients is we define the result the client wants. In the next step we define what it will take to achieve that result. You can list 1 result or a 100. The process is the same. List the result and what it takes to achieve it. Next, think about what obstacles could occur along your results path. Define what it will take to get through these obstacles. You can list one obstacle or a hundred. Whatever the number, just make sure you define them and what it takes to get through them.

Using this process, I find that my clients can finally visualize the results they want. They can see themselves achieving the results before they ever achieve them. I find my clients more willing to work hard and overcome the obstacles along the way to get the results they want because they know what they are working towards.

I know it is hard to believe. I am sure you are asking yourself. "How can changing that one simple word from goals to results make such a difference in one's life?" I believe the word change does something in our brains. We are hardwired to achieve results. We may not be hardwired to achieve goals. What I do know is that my clients are amazed at how a simple act of giving up goals can open up a whole world of achievements. That's why I believe we should give up goals and start working towards results.

"When you think and focus on results then

you get the results that you think and focus on."

Jean Oursler, The Results Queen

About Jean Oursler

Her clients have crowned Jean Oursler the Results Queen because they say she is all about getting the results they want. Jean specializes in Breakthrough Results with entrepreneurs, business owners, accountants, financial planners and lawyers who hate sales and marketing and want their business to grow and thrive.

Her clients make low six-figure new business development sales within the first 12 months or less doing it in a way that makes them feel comfortable.

Are you ready to achieve the Breakthrough RESULTS!?

Contact Jean today!

Websites:

For entrepreneurs: http://www.womengetresults.com

For financial services: http://www.practicemanagement.com

Email: jean@moreresultsnow.com

Chapter 2

Scaling Up – How to Go From Solo to Self-Sustaining

Authored by Donna Miller

There's nothing small about small business. Every minute, a new business is started in the U.S. and according to several professional sources, such as Forbes, LinkedIn, and Business Insider, more than 50% of all workers will be self-employed by 2020. Small businesses lead job creation, and the U.S. Federal government now awards 23% of all contracts to small businesses. Yet, only 4% of small businesses break $1 million in sales, and there is still a 90% failure rate. Ouch.

You started your business or your consulting practice with great plans, strategies, dreams, and hopes. You thought you would make more money, achieve work-life balance, and be the parent (or boss) you always wanted to be. And then the business started to consume your life in ways you never could have imagined. You are now working more hours than ever, not quite making what you thought you would, and that work-life balance has become an unreachable dream that taunts you.

Whether it's just you or you've got a team, how great would it be if your company ran itself? Or, think about how much more you could get done if you only focused on what you love? Here's a hint: the answer to each of those questions is the path to the other.

So, what's a solopreneur to do?

Over the last 21 years, I've gone from being a solopreneur to leading an organization that runs itself while I enjoy real work-life balance. I've been able to travel internationally, work right from the beach, and spend the summer exploring our vast and beautiful country in an RV. Here's the truth: it is unlikely that I will have enough cash in the bank to feel comfortable retiring but, as it turns out, I am not the retiring type. My best investment is the revenue-producing organization I have created.

Bigger is not necessarily better. Everyone needs to find their sweet spot, and scaling up to an organization that doesn't consume you is the path to work-life balance, professional autonomy, and financial freedom. There are many aspects of creating a successful business. Here are a few fundamentals to help you begin your process of scaling up:

1. **Think like an organization to become one.** Take some time to create an organizational chart. Even though it might look like "you, you, you, you" right now, it will be the foundation for building your team of the future. Today your options to "staff up" are better than ever (and more affordable). You can easily have access to top talent on an as-needed basis, as well as work to build team through strategic partnerships. The bottom line is that an organizational chart may not be staffed via traditional methods, and that makes you nimble, cost-efficient, and gives you a solid competitive edge.

As you visualize your team of the future and begin to write job descriptions, get very clear on your mission, values, and vision. This is the barometer for all your team-building decisions. As you consider options, ask yourself if they are aligned with who you are, what you stand for, and where you are going. As Simon Sinek says "hire people who believe what you believe and they will work for you with blood, sweat, and tears." Get clear on what you believe – your *why*.

2. **Begin the process of outsourcing and delegating.** Having created your organizational chart and job descriptions, start by outsourcing the tasks that you absolutely should not be doing. These are tasks that stress you out, are actually forms of procrastination, or you simply have no business doing (admit it – you know you're holding on to a few). Chances are these tasks will include many areas of "administrivia" and especially, bookkeeping. Also, if you can't seem to look away from your phone, social media posting may need to be delegated – this is often a "shiny object" that is really just another form of procrastination.

You are going to come to a point where you cannot afford NOT to get some help. Make that change before you are on the "I can do it myself quicker" hamster wheel – the longer that cycle continues, the harder it is to break.

3. **Focus on driving revenue.** This starts with charging as if you already had a team doing the work, not just you! "Think" in Excel as you build out your pricing structure or write proposals. Make sure you have enough margin from the beginning to hire people or bring partners in to do the work. This also means building in enough margin to cover your cost (salary + benefits) as a fully or partially non-billable expense of running the business.

   You need to focus on what you are uniquely qualified to do, and for most business owners, that means new business development. As you think like an organization and begin outsourcing, you need to follow the money. You need to create a new business development plan that leverages your marketing efforts. Driving revenue should be your number one priority.

4. **Document it all.** As you start delegating, document your processes, and I mean document them ALL (another helpful hint: have the people you are delegating to document it). Create processes and keep it simple. Simple ideas are easy to understand. Ideas that are easy to understand are repeated. Ideas that are repeated create transformation. If you haven't yet read *The E-Myth* by Michael E. Gerber, I promise you, it's a must!

5. **Maintain focus as you expand.** Do not fall prey to the shiny object syndrome. Have your team hold you accountable, work referral sources, and get clear on niche markets or specific verticals. Most importantly, be proactive about your time and make sure the revenue producing tasks are always the first priority.

Perhaps you have just started your business, or you are a few years (or even decades) along in your entrepreneurial journey. Here's a simple truth: the value of applying fundamental business practices, the "Business 101s," never ends.

The reality is, you may have to step back to move forward. Successful companies who scale up stay strategic and here are some fundamental strategic steps:

1. **Planning** – get strategic, do a SWOT analysis (Strengths, Weaknesses, Opportunities, and Threats), ask for help in identifying your blind spots - and we all have them. Document it all!

2. **Execution** – move forward with a clear direction (niche markets and specific verticals) and SMART goals (Specific, Measurable, Attainable, Realistic, Timed). Test, measure, tweak. Continue to update documentation.

3. **Expansion** – once you've got the right formula you can "turn the volume up" to scale your results. Continue to monitor results, change as needed and (drumroll, please)…document it all.

4. **Self-Sustaining** – become the true leader of the organization by giving guidance to your team, focusing on driving revenue, and perfecting the skills that bring you the greatest joy.

Simple, but not necessarily easy. Building a self-sustaining organization is the long-game, and it requires strategy, focus, and consistency.

You've probably heard the phrase "dress for the job you want." In the world of entrepreneurship, that translates to "behave like the organization you want to become." Focus on that which you are uniquely qualified to do and delegate that which takes you away from your genius. Over time, you will build an organization that runs itself while you focus on what you love, and your business will fuel the life of your dreams.

About Donna Miller

Donna is a business and community leader, a speaker, an educator and an entrepreneur who is passionate about seeing small businesses thrive.

Her team has helped well over 1,500 companies to start and grow by providing back office support, bookkeeping, educational programs and office space. She believes in the power of collaboration (C3=Connect, Collaborate, Community) and that companies should be a force for good.

She is the recipient of numerous awards, she is a sought after speaker and in her "spare" time she is Chair of the Salvation Army Advisory Board in Montclair. She is a regular blogger and can often been found on a beach writing.

Contact Donna Today!

Website: http://www.c3workplace.com

Blog: http://www.c3workplace.com/blog

Email: donna@c3workplace.com

Chapter 3

Knowing the Right Experts to Achieve Business Success

Authored by Rose Ríos, MPH

Our history is full of experts who defined government, developed medical breakthroughs, reformed legal systems and created advanced technologies. Some are very well known in contemporary society while others require a study on particular subject matters to understand their contributions and full value. For example, if individuals are asked to name the greatest inventors, icons like Thomas Edison and Alexander Graham Bell will be mentioned. If asked who are the greatest artists of all time? Masters such as Leonardo da Vinci, Paul Gaugin, and Vincent Van Gogh, will likely be cited. If asked about experts in software technology, it is likely they will name Steve Jobs.

Why are these individuals named? What do they all have in common?

They have not only made a significant impact in their field but on society.

However, experts do not have to be internationally recognized and mentioned with historical significance. We often seek the assistance of experts to complete various tasks. We pursue medical specialists to treat specific illnesses, we reach out to building contractors for home improvement projects, we contact attorneys to navigate the legal system, and we even look up the recipes of a particular chef to make a fantastic meal for guests. Our outreach to experts often occurs, maybe even every day.

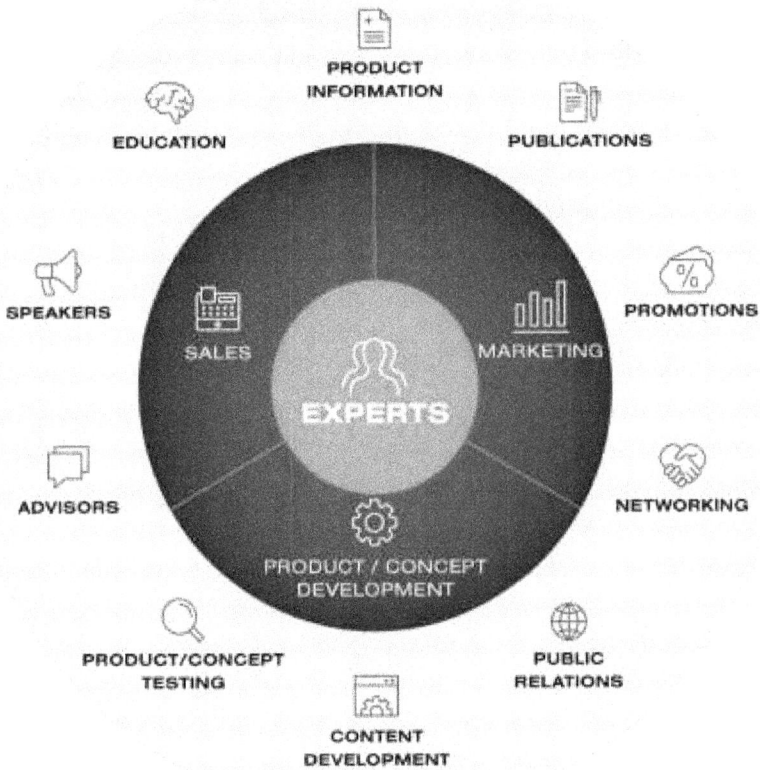

The reasons we reach out to experts are numerous, yet the ultimate reason is to accomplish a task successfully. These tasks could be brand new, or are tasks we have tried before, but ended with poor results. We also reach out to experts because we are often required to work on multiple tasks that mandate our attention. Many studies show that email addiction has become an epidemic. We are working more hours, spending less time with family and forsaking even our most basic healthcare needs. We also tend to work on areas that address our strengths versus our weaknesses, because it is easy or something familiar. It becomes a habit and moving out of the comfort zone becomes a challenge. Therefore, we rely on the use of experts to help us accomplish goals and reach success.

We choose experts based on their demonstrated capability and knowledge skill. This may come in the form of experts getting published, winning awards, or receiving media recognition. Overall, it requires behavior to be prolific, consistent, and visible. We may know experts because we have witnessed them being interviewed on television and labeled as one; or perhaps they create their own visibility and profess their expertise. Regardless of how the expertise is recognized, the important thing is it is recognized.

Beyond using experts to help with personal tasks, various types of expertise can also be used to run a business. Successfully running a business requires not just an idea, but the execution of that idea with knowledge and skill. Managing an enterprise is hard work, and an entrepreneur cannot do it all alone. Entrepreneurs may often have initial roles as sales, marketer, as well as overseeing operations and resource management.

However, success is dependent on the entrepreneurs knowing their areas of strength and identifying experts to work on those areas that address their weaknesses or lack of knowledge in a particular skill. This is why businesses have departments for specialized skills, including marketing, human resources, finance, operations, information technology, etc.

Identifying experts is very much like performing a job interview, but it is more important to first understand particular areas of need and even improvement. The more detailed and specific the need, the more likely you can find an expert to accomplish your goals. This information is also of value to measure the success of the required actions in reaching your business goals.

It may be necessary to identify more than one expert if there are multiple needs or the scope of what needs to be accomplished is large. For example, a project might call for more experts with a larger geographic scope. It is essential to understand the scope of the need to accurately identify the type and number of experts.

I often get requests from clients to identify medical experts. They will tell me they need one hundred international experts. I ask questions about the disease area, what type of criteria the experts should possess, and how they are going to use the experts to determine with more accuracy if the number should be modified to more or less. For example, I once had a client who needed medical experts in Alzheimer's disease. There are easily about one hundred experts working in that area in the United States alone. They lead clinical trials nationally, write publications, and present their results at major medical conferences all over the world. However, when speaking to the client about his particular need, I discovered what he really wanted were experts who used digital imaging in the diagnosis of Alzheimer's disease and mapping the progression of the ailment. The list quickly decreased from one hundred to eight.

Once you have recognized the scope of need, the next step is to know how you will use the experts. Beyond their knowledge or skill, do they need to take your product or service to another level, present your product, or demonstrate the company's innovation and commitment to the industry or task? Do they need to know how to navigate social media and or submit articles for publishing consideration? Finding the use for experts is very much like writing a job description. Take into consideration how you need the expert to work to accomplish your business goals. Can the expert meet those requirements and how have they demonstrated their skill in the past?

Knowing the scope of need and the activities required of the expert will help define how to identify the expert. If looking for an expert to promote products, it is necessary to identify someone who has a dynamic personality and commands the attention of your target audience. If your business goals require the need to increase your market presence through publications, then identify prolific authors on specific topics in trade and peer-reviewed journals.

There are a number of questions to ask yourself before picking an expert. Can this expert affect change? Does the expert garner the respect and recognition of his/her peers? Is the expert cited/quoted? Has this individual received an award, been interviewed or labeled as creator/innovator in that industry?

You may be fortunate enough to hire experts as full-time staff members. However, some businesses are forced to use them as consultants. Since that particular expert is so successful, he or she has created a business of outsourcing themselves. The question is then focused on how to partner with the expert. One of the greatest benefits of the Internet today, (as well as most alarming) is the wealth of information you can find on someone. Various social media and networking sites are infamous for being conduits of identification of lost loved ones, high school buddies, and of course, experts. These sites present opportunities for engagement and partnership.

Sometimes the initial contact can be as simple as a phone call or email. Other times, it can require innovative approaches. Are there conferences or trade shows where your expert will be in attendance? Do you know someone who is in the same network as the expert that can provide an introduction?

One of my friends just landed a job as an outreach coordinator for a non-profit group. She was tasked with the responsibility of performing focus groups so the organization can develop educational materials and seek resources to help patients manage their care. This seems like a very noble job function. However, her organization was funded by pharmaceutical companies, and this was perceived negatively by patients. These patients wanted the use of services but did not want to participate in any market research in fear that their information will be shared with the pharmaceutical companies, which in turn would try to push their branded medications. Together, we identified a closed social media group, which consisted of the patients my friend wished to work with. We contacted the organizers of the group, shared with them the survey. It was clear that the organizers were experts in various aspects of managing their care, and therefore, were an excellent resource for my friend. She shared with them her duties and end goal. In turn, they shared with her their fears but also what they needed from the organization to ensure their privacy was protected. It turned out to not only be a great working partnership but one that developed with multiple stakeholders over time.

The use of an expert may be a single encounter, or a constant working partnership for innovation development, product promotion, and education. If the latter, it is necessary to evaluate the partnerships to determine continued success or develop mitigation strategies as needed. There may be times that the expert has lost visibility, and peer recognition or others have instead garnered more notoriety.

To remain on the edge of innovation, it may be necessary to assess the peer recognition of your experts and reevaluate other candidates. A high-level executive at a well-known technology company contacted me stating that the company was losing market shares and wanted me to uncover probable factors. My company developed and distributed a survey and discovered that the expert this technology company was contracting did not have the same breadth of peer recognition as he had previously. He was seen as being too financially focused and potentially biased by his selected financial supporters. Our survey also requested nominations of experts with a particular set of skills, previously defined with the client. The nominations were validated, and the client was provided with recommendations of which experts to engage, when to contact them, and how to work with them. The technology company incorporated these recommendations into its business plan and saw an eighteen percent rise in market share the next year.

Therefore, when seeking the assistance of an expert to achieve business success, follows these simple tips:

1. Identify the area of your business that requires the use of an expert

2. Be as detailed as possible in your need

3. Develop a list of criteria that the expert must possess to meet your business need

4. Evaluate accomplishments and mitigate as needed

Bottom line, running a business is not just about what you know, but who also you know.

About Rose Ríos

Rose Ríos has a wealth of experience in many aspects of health care, including qualitative market research; agency-side medical communications; and direct patient care, advocacy, and education. For the past fifteen years, she has worked on identifying thought leaders in various therapeutic areas at the international, national, regional, and local level.

After receiving her degree in medical anthropology from the University of Vermont, Ms. Ríos worked as a bilingual Public Assistance Specialist, serving the medically needy, and then as a Substance Abuse Counselor with HIV/AIDS patients at a methadone maintenance clinic in Brooklyn, NY. She later accepted a position as a Pharmaceutical Sales Representative with Hoffmann-La Roche. During her tenure there, she completed her Master's Degree in Public Health at City University of New York, Hunter College, specializing in Epidemiology and Community Health Education. She is also a certified Emergency Medical Technician.

To identify experts to reach your business success contact Rose:

Contact Rose Today!

Email: rose@kolcomm.net

Phone: 908-912-8980

Chapter 4

Breakthrough! From Money Anxiety to Money Mastery

Authored by Wei Houng

"For things to reveal themselves to us, we need to be ready to

abandon our views about them."

– Thich Nhat Hanh

What does it mean to have a "Breakthrough" in business or life? You hear people talk about it all the time and yet, many people don't even realize just how powerful an actual breakthrough in either business or life can be.

Imagine that there is this wall on the outskirts of your world of reality, that world where all you believe is currently possible. On the other side of that wall is the "other" world, a world of "dreams" and "desires."

That's the world where, in your mind, you have conversations with yourself that go something like this:

"Does that exist? Maybe…no…impossibly…no…well

…maybe for others…but NOT for me and NOT in my world."

For some, it's a world of imagination and beauty. For others, it's completely impossible, and not even worth imagining.

Whatever it is, know that there is a huge wall. That wall is a big part of the reason why people want a "Breakthrough."

And it's a wall where a door may or may not even exist.

If it does, it's locked down with a door forged of an ironclad super-titanium material combined with other out-of-the-world elements. And as if that wasn't enough, this door is also being guarded by an intimidating crew of gatekeepers, creatures, and monsters that, 99% of the time, will make you literally turn and run the other way out of fear every time you attempt to breach the wall.

A "Breakthrough" is achieving the 1%. That one moment …that one time…where either you and/or your cavalry confront all the demons, creatures, and guardians of the aforementioned gate and break through that wall to expand your horizons.

What's so amazing is that when you break through one part of this wall of your current reality, it then weakens all the other parts of the wall that stretches into the horizon of your mind. The walls then become so weak that it crumbles and rebuilds to match and expand your new limits of reality. Those are the new limits that re-define all that is possible.

To put it simply, when you have a Breakthrough in one area of life, the ripple effects are so TREMENDOUS that it impacts and IMPROVES all other areas of your life.

THAT is the power of a "Breakthrough," and THAT is why you want one.

Question is, are you ready for it?

Meet John the Consultant

When John first came to me for help, his business was in a holding pattern.

He had already been running his own business as an entrepreneur for several years, and despite those years as an expert in the field of consulting, along with a long list of client successes, his business had stopped growing. His annual revenues were well into the mid six-figure range, but for some reason he still struggled financially.

Aside from his struggles with money, it turned out that other areas of his life were not all that great either. His marriage was on the rocks because of the financial stress and amount of hours he was putting into his business. He was spending a lot of money on his health because he was constantly having physiological issues due to the stress and worry. His friendships had dwindled down to just a handful of people that he would sporadically have happy hour moments with, which almost always resulted in a hangover the next day due to excessive consumption of alcohol.

He believed, at the time, that the answer to all his problems was to make more money and break the seven-figure mark for his business so that all his "problems" would go away.

When he realized that the bulk of his issues in both business and life were a result of money anxiety, that realization sparked the beginning of a breakthrough journey that literally changed his life by changing his relationship with money.

During the Breakthrough Session to release his money anxiety, it turned out that he had not only adopted bad habits from how his parents dealt with money during his childhood, but he had swathed all the emotions around his childhood experiences of being bullied into the mix as well.

It had created such a massive wall of fear and negative motivators that when we finally broke through, he was physically unrecognizable by his wife and peers due to the level of release and awareness that he had achieved. He had become more relaxed, calmer, and most importantly, more forgiving of himself.

He was, quite literally, a new man.

The results?

He saved his marriage. He reconnected with lost friendships. And since then, has found a new appreciation for a consistent health and fitness regiment. As a nice byproduct, he shattered the seven-figure glass ceiling for his business with grace and ease.

What is Money Anxiety?

One of my coaches once told me:

"Worry and anxiety pushes what you want

further away from you."

- Sheevaun Moran

Money anxiety is best described as an unconscious behavior that runs on autopilot when one is confronted with any decision-making process that has a connection with money, value, or survival.

It has a tendency to exist in cultures and societies that utilize some representation of money that can be exchanged for products or services. The reason that is is because when a culture utilizes a universal medium to facilitate commerce, it requires the people to have a dissociated attachment to the product or service itself which, by its very nature, eliminates a big part of why people buy things to begin with.

Almost nobody ever buys anything unemotionally. The ultimate catalyst that pushes one over the final threshold to reach into one's wallet to pay for something is usually an emotional one.

For example, if you were to shop or buy the perfect gift for someone you love, is it the gift or the money spent on that gift that holds the most value for you when you decide to purchase it?

The money simply facilitates it, right?

If we get caught up on how much that one gift costs, are we now trying to attach a value to our expression of love and affection for that person? Are we now then attaching a value to our love?

Yes, money anxiety can put us in a very vicious cycle…IF we let it.

The source of our money anxiety almost always comes as a result of our relationship with money.

That relationship has been forged over the course of time from our experiences with the people and events in our life.

It comes from Who, Where, When, and How:

- We learned to deal with money.

- We learned to think about money.

- We learned to define what money is.

- We learned what role to give money in our life.

And depending on WHO you learned from, WHERE you learned it, WHEN you learned it, and HOW you were taught, these are all ingredients that contribute to your money anxiety.

What is Money Mastery?

It's really more about how we define Money Mastery. Take with a grain of salt what the "money gurus" of the world tell us. We are too often caught up with the belief that money is the way to determine our value in the world we live in. The irony is that as soon as we let that belief go, money flows into our lives as easily as water out of a faucet.

Mastering money is about mastering your own value. The clearer you are with what your value is and why you do what you do, the easier it is for money to reflect that worth. To say that your value is priceless is an understatement of epic proportions. Consider this quote from one of my mentors:

"Whatever you think you are, you are more than that."

- Dr. Matt James

The best thing about that statement is that it leads to a limitless path of constant growth because just when you think you've "arrived," you'll realize that you are even more so.

When you master money, money starts to truly work for you, and not just to make you more money; it works for you in a symbiotic way to help you achieve and create the life you truly want.

Uncovering Your Money Truth

This is the crucial step that most people skip. A step that when skipped, is the main reason money anxiety keeps showing up in the most inopportune places of your business and life.

Anyone who has done any level of personal development will, at one point or another, be confronted with the task of "facing the mirror" to acknowledge the truth behind the obstacles they keep avoiding to address.

Exposing the unconscious truth of why money anxiety runs its old programs in your life will reveal the specific leverage points of extraction. In this particular case, the truth WILL set you free.

So what I'm going to do is explain a little bit about how the following process is designed to uproot the origins of your beliefs and patterns around money so that you can confront, embrace, and release the ones that no longer serve you.

What you can then do is use the exercise to start revealing what could potentially change the way you make and create prosperity in your life…to give you the Breakthrough Results around money and prosperity you're looking for.

The exercise is really quite simple when done properly. It's simple because it is structured to allow your unconscious mind (where the behavioral and emotional programs dwell) to answer the questions in the most revealing and honest way possible.

You can, of course, fool and lie to yourself to avoid the truth, but what would be the point since the results of the exercise is really for nobody else but you?

What you are going to do is get a blank sheet of paper and give knee-jerk type IMMEDIATE answers to the following questions. The key is to do it as FAST as you can with the first words that come to mind so your adult and conscious filters don't have a chance to think about what the "right" answers should be.

Your goal is to be unabashedly honest with the answers so that you can reveal the reason(s) why you aren't where you want to be regarding money, abundance, and prosperity.

Ready? Here we go…

1. What does Money mean to you?

2. Why is Money important to you?

3. How do you know when you HAVE enough?

4. How do you know when you ARE enough?

5. What is your biggest FEAR around Money?

6. How was Money handled at home while you were growing up?

7. People with lots of money are _____

8. In order to have more money, I would need to _____

This should be a good start. You should take no longer than one to two minutes to answer ALL the questions. It needs to be that quick. Any longer and you've already started filtering it through the filters of Money Anxiety to keep the truth hidden.

Once you're done with the exercise, you can then go through and start asking yourself how you knew to answer the questions the way you did and where you learned the beliefs that drove those answers. Taking the time to really meditate on that usually reveals some life-changing revelations.

Take those revelations and apply any of the myriad release techniques Breakthrough coaches use to release the ones that no longer serve you and your business.

If you do this exercise properly, be prepared to have some amazing Breakthrough results!

About Wei Houng

Money Anxiety Breakthrough Coach and Speaker, Wei Houng, is a founding member of The 6 Figure Academy and has made it his passion, purpose, and goal to help entrepreneurs eliminate anxiety about money to achieve financial success and live a prosperous and abundant lifestyle.

For over 15 years, his desire to help others achieve financial enlightenment has evolved into a symbiotic adventure for both him, his team and his clients. He has worked with celebrities, industry thought leaders, and thousands of entrepreneurs to re-define the role that money plays in their lives. The results have been life changing for his students and clients.

To learn more about how to break through your money anxiety and MASTER money as an entrepreneur go to http://the6figure academy.com/breakthrough-results-book for a *Breakthrough Results* book exclusive gift.

Contact Wei Today!

Website: http://the6figureacademy.com/breakthrough-results-book

Chapter 5

Healthy Credit, Better You

Authored by Denise A. Cestone

"Success is the sum of small efforts, repeated day in and day out."

Robert Collier

Congratulations for taking this essential step toward creating and soon to be enjoying what it is to have an outstanding credit score and all the well-deserved freedom that comes along with it. Of the many who talk about cleaning up their credit report, clearly, since you are reading this, you are one of the very few who take real action. Because of that, you will have breakthrough results and enjoy all the rewards that go along with it. My top three strategies are a unique, revolutionary approach that contain my expert strategies combined with psychology. These strategies have guided my private clients to achieve a greater state of financial health than they ever imagined. If you have ever felt discouraged, hopeless or that your life is too busy to figure how to increase your credit score, then hold on. In just a few days you will be amazed at what is possible for you as it relates to increasing your credit score.

The Top 3 Quick Start Strategies I Learned From Working At The Credit Bureaus To Increase Your Credit Score FAST! They are:

1. The Real Secret to a High Credit Score – Your Why.

2. The Power of You - Your Actions.

3. Living Life – Your Results.

These strategies are nothing like you've seen before. It's about getting something that's deeper. Something that at the very root controls not only your credit score, but every detail of your life. It's about tapping into your why, your deeper power, the power that drives you to do what you do to get results.

Strategy #1: The Real Secret to a High Credit Score – Your Why.

You are embarking on a journey to take action towards increasing and maintaining a high credit score once and for all so you can reclaim and live the life you fully deserve. It's about getting your mojo back and freeing yourself up to experience more joy and happiness that having a high credit score can provide to you and your family.

Your credit score will begin to improve as you become increasingly happy. Did you know your emotion is the most power force in the universe? When you learn how to align your emotions, take advantage of them and feel the experience, you will take action towards your goal. In this case, it's to improve your overall credit report.

Why do you do the things you do? Why do you say you will pay your bills on time, but then pay them late? Or why do you say you will pay off all your bills to a zero balance, but go out shopping? One reason is you are exhausted and feel hopeless. You are tired from all the stress and pressure of daily living and all the things you are dealing with inside.

Your energy has power. If you do not have energy, it's very hard to take the necessary action. We have to rebuild that energy. We have to make mental and emotional shifts to release the trapped energy inside you so you will take action on the necessary steps to improve your credit score.

So I ask you, "Why?"

Why do you want to clean up your credit and increase your credit score? Is it to purchase a house for you and your family? Is it to get a job? A better rate on your insurances? To sleep better at night? What is it? What's your "Why?" Write it out on a piece of paper. Do you feel it in your gut, your heart, and soul? Does it make you want to take action? If not, stop and continue to write out your "Why?" until it does.

If your "Why?" is powerful to you, then the following is your first assignment.

Get your current credit report, including credit scores directly from the three major credit bureaus.

There are three major credit reporting agencies that will offer you one free credit report per year. You will have to pay a fee to get your score, though. I strongly recommend you do so to have a baseline of your credit score. The credit bureaus are:

Equifax: http://www.equifax.com, 1-800-685-1111.

TransUnion: at http://www.transunion.com, 1-877-322-8228.

Experian: http://www.experian.com, call 888 397 3742.

Most of the time when you download your credit report, you will be able to view and save it instantly. Save it to your computer's document file if you can. That way you'll be able to print it out and refer to it as much as you need.

Congratulations! You've completed the first step towards increasing your credit score. You know your "Why?" and have your current credit report including your score. You should feel an increased amount of energy knowing you are taking the necessary actions. Celebrate yourself for this. Reread your "Why?" I bet it's juicy and has meaning. Are you beginning to feel more powerful? Then get ready for Strategy #2, The Power of You − Your Actions.

Strategy #2 The Power of You − Your Actions

Do you truly understand the power of you and who you really are? The six human needs (Certainty, Variety, Significance, Connection/Love, Growth, and Contribution), are the most powerful and versatile tools we can use to create lasting change in our lives. When you understand your top two needs, you'll be able to access and know the true power of you.

Assignment #2 is to write down what of the six human needs are your top two. Is it Certainty and Significance? Growth and Contribution? Study them and understand them. This will reinforce the power of you, keep you committed to your "Why?" while continuing to take action.

Now that you have your current credit report, apply some strategies to lift your score.

The overall mantra for getting and maintaining a high credit score is to pay your bills on time, keep account balances low, and take out new credit only when you need it. People who do that faithfully have very high scores. It usually means you're conservative and cautious about credit. If that were already the case, you probably wouldn't be reading this.

An initial powerful, quick strategy to concentrate on is **Correcting Errors**.

Look for errors such as accounts that aren't yours, late payments that were paid on time, debts you paid off that are shown as outstanding, old debts that shouldn't be reported any longer and inquiries you never authorized.

Some areas to check and correct that most people don't know about are account mix ups because you are a JR, and another family member is a SR, accounts that are no longer yours because of a divorce or some other situation, name, address, job and date of birth variations.

Remember, if it's on your credit report, it's in the calculation. Ensure everything you see is correct.

Negatives are supposed to be deleted after seven years, except bankruptcies, which can stay for as long as ten years.

Sign back into your online credit bureau account and follow the dispute instructions.

Bonus Strategies

Are your accounts in the proper categories? The Following are the definitions.

Real Estate: First and second mortgage loans on your home.

Installment: Accounts comprised of fixed terms with regular payments, such as a car loan.

Revolving: Accounts with opened terms with varying payments, such as a credit card account.

Collection: Accounts seriously past due that have been assigned to an attorney or collection agency.

Other: Accounts where the exact category is unknown. This could include 30-day accounts, such as an American Express card. Correct the ones that are not properly coded.

Check your limits. Your score might be artificially depressed if your lender is showing a lower limit than you've actually got. Most credit-card issuers will quickly update this information if you ask.

If your issuer makes it a policy not to report consumers' limits, however, as is the usual case with American Express cards and those issued by Capital One. The bureaus typically use your highest balance as a proxy for your credit limit.

You may see the problem here: If you consistently charge the same amount each month − say $2,000 to $2,500 − it may look to the credit-scoring formula like you're regularly maxing out that card.

Check your last statement to see which day of the month your account closes, then go to the issuer's Web site a week in advance of closing and pay off what you owe. It won't raise your reported limit, but it will widen the gap between that limit and your closing balance, which should boost your score.

Dust off an old card. The older your credit history, the better. If you stop using your oldest cards, the issuers may stop updating those accounts at the credit bureaus. The accounts will still appear, but they won't be given as much weight in the credit-scoring formula as your active accounts. That's why I recommend to my clients to use their oldest cards every few months to charge a small amount, paying it off in full when the statement arrives.

Get some goodwill. If you've been a good customer, a lender might agree to erase that one late payment from your credit history. You usually have to make the request in writing, and your chances for a "goodwill adjustment" improve the better your record with the company (and the better your credit in general). But it can't hurt to ask.

Strategy # 3 Living Life – Your Results

You've done it. Now you are ready to live life with passion, confidence, power, and energy, free from any prior embarrassment you may have made. You completed the major necessary steps, took action and learned a few things along the way. Now it's a function of time before you see your credit score increase. That can be anywhere from 30 – 90 days or longer depending on the complexity of your repairs.

Credit is an important part of our society and your life. Cherish yourself, your credit history and your credit score. Make it just as important to you as you are and keep it clean and pristine. Stay focused on your "Why?" It will never let you down.

If you're ready for more techniques and strategies on how to continue to increase and maintain your credit score, visit us at http://www.IncreaseYourCreditScore.Org to receive your free gift.

About Denise A. Cestone

Founder and CEO of Increase Your Credit Score, LLC, Denise is a nationally recognized expert on Fixing Credit Scores, Credit Repair, Credit Scoring and Debt Reduction.

Denise works exclusively with Consumers, Mortgage Professionals and Real Estate Professionals focusing on increasing credit scores so they can get what they want...FAST.

Known for her Bottom Line results and the ability to laser focus on what will yield her clients the highest results in the shortest amount of time, it's no surprise she is known to them as "their secret weapon" to increasing credit scores fast.

Denise has an MBA in Finance and Economics and over 25 years' experience in the credit industry, including positions with TransUnion, American Express, Citibank and NCO Financial Systems Inc. Denise's desire is to get people what they want...FAST!

Contact Denise Today!

Website: http://www.IncreaseYourCreditScore.Org

Email: Info@IncreaseYourCreditScore.Org

Twitter: https://twitter.com/FixMyCreditFast

Facebook: https://www.facebook.com/Denise.Cestone

LinkedIn: https://www.linkedin.com/in/denisecestone

Chapter 6

Understanding Consumer Perception

Authored by Rachel Durkan

Webster defines perception as "the action or faculty of perceiving; cognition; an immediate or intuitive recognition as of a moral or aesthetic quality; a single unified meaning obtained from sensory processes while a stimulus is present.

Perception is how we understand or interpret an idea, concept or thing. You have likely heard that perception is reality; how we each perceive something makes it real.

In his book "Blink," Malcolm Gladwell wrote that even slight changes, additions, and tweaks to packaging of certain products changed how people reacted to them. When researches added 15% more yellow to green on 7UP® packaging, consumers reported that it had more lime than lemon flavor, even though the drink was not changed.

In another study, experts found when they used a close-up picture of a real human face on a can of Chef Boyardee® Ravioli, consumers perceived increased quality more than if the company used a full body shot or a cartoon character.

Our five senses help us identify and conceptualize everything we hear, taste, smell, feel and see. When we perceive an idea or thing, we experience an immediate or intuitive recognition. Two people look at a paint swatch: one person sees a deep blue, the other sees purple. Both have formed an opinion based on what they actually see. Who is right? Both, because they each have formed an opinion based on one of their sensory perceptions.

Perception is *Everything*

Launching a new business that delivers a product or service is exciting, because as a business owner, you know that your winning idea is a slam-dunk. How could it not be? You have asked family and friends for their feedback, and they endorsed your venture

100%. Perhaps some of those people may have even invested in your new business, which skyrockets your confidence into the stratosphere. Just think, if launching a successful business were that easy, we all would be wildly successful entrepreneurs and have no need to learn how to improve our products, services or businesses. However, eight of ten new businesses fail. According to Forbes Magazine the top five reasons that the failure rate is so high are:

1. **Entrepreneurs are not in touch with their customers through deep dialogue**. Entrepreneurs who have not clearly identified what their customers like, need or want are missing important information. Just because you believe a product or service is a "must-have" does not mean your target audience will see value in it. Did you ask your potential customer if they perceive your product or service as valuable?

2. **Consumers don't discern a difference between your offerings and what is already available in the marketplace.** Your product does not have a unique value proposition.

3. **Business owners fail to communicate the value propositions to their market in a clear, concise, compelling fashion.** Perhaps as an entrepreneur, you don't have consumer-friendly

marketing materials that explain the value of your offering. Maybe you, (the owner) are brilliant but you lack the social and communication skills needed to convert shoppers into buyers.

4. Sometimes there is **a breakdown in leadership**. That's right — the founder is dysfunctional. He or she may have built an organizational culture that fosters secrecy, disorganization and non-cooperation. Each leader sets the tone for everyone in the organization.

5. The entrepreneur **lacks the ability to develop a profitable business model with proven revenue streams**. Just because the head honcho thinks his idea is going to change the world, that doesn't mean anyone else will buy into it.

We can attribute the first three items (and possibly the fourth) to a lack of perception. In most cases, small business owners assume they know what makes their product or service valuable because after all, *they love it!*

Let's say, Chef Tom, executive chef at a famous area restaurant, is bored with his mushroom soup recipe. Even though it is one of Tom's bestsellers, he wants to "improve" it and thinks his customers will love it. When the new "Chef Tom's Mushroom Soup" made it onto the menu, customers tried it and hated it. Tom's customers wanted to enjoy the soup they had been sipping for years, not something new! If Chef Tom had taken the time to ask his customers if they were tired of the old recipe, he would have known that he should not have tinkered with the "old" soup. After two months on the menu and throwing out gallons of soup every day, Chef Tom brought back the customer's favorite soup, and it is back to being a bestseller.

Consider a bookkeeper who takes pride in being a detail-oriented financial expert who never rushes through a spreadsheet. Sounds good, right? But, what if her clients have deadlines and want their financials turned over quickly; they don't have time for a bookkeeper who checks his or her numbers three times to make sure they are correct. The bookkeeper will see her attention to detail as her value add, but the consumer will perceive the delay negatively.

These two entrepreneurs are creative, talented and special, but they failed to identify their value to the target market. They both needed to conduct studies, focus groups, and/or interviews to gain feedback on their products and practices to better understand how the consumer perceives them. The chef failed to consider his customers' opinions when he revised his soup recipe, and the accountant didn't consider her clients' value of timeliness over detail.

When you understand how your target market perceives your product or service (their reality) and learn what factors are most important to them, you gain the ability to better position your product or service in such a way that it will appear most valuable to your target audience. It is a win-win situation when you know what truly makes your customers happy.

Case Study

A few years ago, one of my clients (let's call him GoodGuy LLC) identified a need for a software tool that would automate Human Resource initiatives in large organizations.

GoodGuy was excited about the project and hired a project manager and development team to create the software. Before long, the software (which incorporated innovative and fun features in an easy-to-use program) was ready to launch. GoodGuy spent hundreds of thousands of dollars because he knew this product was a winner. GoodGuy had excellent relationships with several local Fortune 500 companies and reached out to them first. Four months later, they hadn't made any sales. What happened?

GoodGuy contacted us to help them understand why the company's product sales did not match his projections. After some market research and interviews with potential users to see what they wanted, we found our client had focused on delivering the software *they* thought the consumer needed instead of what the target audience really wanted. They failed to identify customer needs and explore industry trends or competitors' offerings.

We took GoodGuy back to the drawing board and identified the demand in their target market. We found that customers wanted a software with different capabilities. GoodGuy invested more time and money to revise the software and tweak his product. Now, his business was selling something the customer actually wanted. Unfortunately, the product revision took so much time that when the second launch took place, the market was saturated with similar products and GoodGuy missed a huge opportunity. The moral of the story is <u>never assume you know what your customer wants.</u>

It is important to remember that every customer cares about two things:

1. Can you solve my problem or fulfill my need/want?

2. Can you solve my problem or fulfill my need/want better than the competition?

Successful businesses communicate their values simply and concisely. Sometimes a business' key players are too technical and too close to the product, to know how to explain (in consumer-friendly terms) the benefits of their product or service.

Our World is Changing – What Influences Consumer Perceptions Today?

Change is inevitable and social media has changed how we live, how we think and how we consume. Let's look at some new facts and figures[1]:

- Your pet goldfish has a longer attention span than your customer. The attention span of your customer is seven seconds; the goldfish can focus for eight seconds.

- Over the next ten years, 40% of brands we know today will be gone.

- More than fifty percent of the population is under 30.

- More people own a mobile device than have a toothbrush.

- Social media influences ninety-three percent of shoppers' buying decisions.

- **Seventy-eight percent of today's consumers trust recommendations from their peers, whereas, fourteen percent trust recommendations from advertisements.**

- Only eighteen percent of television advertisements generate a positive ROI.

- Thirty-four percent of bloggers post opinions about products and brands.

Social media has dramatically increased the speed in which customers learn about new products and services. Today, more than ever, it is important to communicate a clear message and encourage brand advocates to reinforce that message to ensure a brand is correctly perceived. Since everyone has a slightly different perception of value, making sure brand perceptions are accurate is more important (and challenging) than ever.

Luckily for businesses, usually there is an industry trend, and to be successful, it is important to identify the core needs/wants of the masses. In doing so, business owners must "walk the talk." Remember that 78% of today's consumers trust peer recommendations. This means that how others perceive one's brand, product or service will quickly determine the brand's success or failure. If a business promises something and doesn't deliver, the world will know it.

The Solution? Simply Ask

If understanding the customers' wants and needs were easy, each new business would be a wild success. The challenge of understanding the customer's perception has brought even the largest corporations to their knees.

To ensure that your product/service and marketing message is being perceived correctly simply ask your audience. This seems like a simple concept, but many business owners and marketing directors neglect to do it thoroughly. Don't underestimate the importance of conducting research and engaging in a continuous, deep dialogue with the target audience to ensure that the business and its customers are perceiving things in the same manner. By keeping in touch with the target audience via surveys, social media conversations, research, and reviews, businesses can ensure their customer's perceptions have not changed.

Simply put, for a business to be successful it is essential that the organization understands and delivers what the consumer really wants, not what *the business owner thinks their customer* wants. Every business's success is based on positioning the value of a product or service in a way the will resonate with the target audience.

---

[1] #socialnomics 2014 by Erik Qualman.
https://www.youtube.com/watch?v=zxpa4dNVd3c

About Rachel Durkan

Rachel Durkan is the founder of Paradigm Marketing and Design (PMD), a full-service marketing and branding agency that offers marketing strategy development and execution, and creative services.

As a recent winner of three Graphic Design Awards from GDUSA – two for website design and one for print – PMD is unique in that it integrates a client's entire marketing strategy to be cohesive and ensure that each marketing initiative (brand development, website design, communication initiatives, etc.) supports a strategic plan to promote business growth. Paradigm has served hundreds of clients in a wide variety of industries including nonprofit, consumer goods and services, technology and energy, and professional services.

Before launching Paradigm, Rachel worked at Pfizer then United Way. She holds an MBA from Fairleigh Dickenson University and certifications in website development and graphic design.

Rachel lives in New Jersey with her husband and their son. Rachel has a passion for both traveling and volunteering and has spent time working in Tanzania, Costa Rica and right here in the United States supporting different philanthropic endeavors.

Contact Rachel Today!

Website: http://www.paradigmmarketinganddesign.com

Email: rjdurkan@paradigmmarketinganddesign.com

Phone: 973-998-5050

Facebook: https://www.facebook.com/rjdevelopmentllc

Twitter: https://twitter.com/ParadigmMDesign

LinkedIn: https://www.linkedin.com/company/rj-development-llc?trk=cp_followed_name_rj-development-llc

Chapter 7

Write Well, Get Noticed: 17 Tips for Writing Awesome Content

Authored by Sue Toth

Conflicting messages about content abound all over the Internet. On the one hand, we're told that humans have an attention span of about eight seconds, a second shorter than a goldfish! On the other hand, we're also constantly bombarded with messages that "content is king." You have to have content, people want to know all about you…and on it goes. What's a business owner to do?

You're going to heed both of these warnings, actually. "But how?" you may ask. You're going to use the words you need to use, but present them in such a way that your reader will see them, read them, and pay attention to them. Your readers will get what they want, which is information about you and your business, and you'll get what you want, which is increased sales for your business. Ready for a win/win? Okay, let's go.

1. **Know Your Customer:** Before you even put pen to paper (or fingers to keyboard), you need to make sure you know your customers, I mean, really know them. Who are they? Where do they hang out? What do they like to do? How do they spend their money? What are they looking for before they buy? What are they looking for from you? Gather all of this information before you start writing anything. Take notes. Make yourself a profile of your best customers, so that you know how to serve them, and you can target your words to their needs.

2. **Plan, Plan, Plan:** Now that you know your customers, you can start targeting your messages right to them. You've figured out what they need. Now figure out how and when they need it. Plan your messaging ahead by using an editorial calendar. If you Google the term "editorial calendar," you'll come up with a wealth of templates that you can use. Once you've found one

you like, fill it in. Go at least six months in advance, even a year if possible. You can always add to it at the last minute if need be, but once you have a basic plan in place, you won't be scrambling at the last minute trying to think of what you're going to say in your blog this month.

3. **Be Timely:** When you're planning, of course you'll want to plan your promotions around holidays, special days, whatever fits your business model and your customer base. But what about those months when there isn't something special to talk about? Do some research. Find timely topics related to your business, and write about them. Check out studies about your product, funny celebration days related to your industry (National Grammar Day is a big one for me), or anything else your customers might want to know. You can fill in those blank spots on your editorial calendar with information that will be relevant to your customers and their needs.

4. **Time To Write:** Now that you're armed with all this pertinent information, you're ready actually to start writing. When you do, pretend that you're chatting with a friend. Be conversational to a certain degree. You should write the way you talk. That doesn't

mean you can go off on tangents. Get to the point, but do so in a friendly manner that your customers will relate to. They want to know you, so use your special style to charm them.

5. **Start With an Attention Grabbing Headline:** You want to draw your readers in with the very first words you say. Wow them at the very beginning of your piece, and you've almost guaranteed they will continue reading. Bore them, and they may move along to something more exciting or interesting.

6. **Don't Be Salesy:** Remember that getting customers is all about building relationships. If you write the equivalent of "buy my product" over and over again, even if you use slightly different ways to say it, you won't get too far with your customers. You know how you don't like to be pushed when you're shopping for something? Your customers don't either. You want to provide information with a call to action, not a sales pitch.

7. **Provide Value:** Don't forget, customers most likely have a lot of places they can go to buy what you are selling. You have to set yourself apart by offering them something just a little extra. It might be a free white paper or free shipping or some extra tips on your website about how best to use your product or service.

Giving away a little bit of knowledge or something for free will help you gain your customers' trust and goodwill.

8. **Don't Use Jargon:** Most industries have a set of terms that are frequently used and well known by those who work in that industry. That doesn't mean your customers will know their meaning! When you're writing, make sure you use language that anyone will understand, no matter how much or little they know about your industry.

9. **Don't Forget Your SEO:** You want to be sure that you show up at the top of the search engines, so you want to include SEO keywords in your writing. You can use tools to help you figure out the best keywords for your product or service. You can also hire a specialist to help you with your SEO needs. Once you've figured out what the best search terms for your website are, use them throughout your content.

10. **But Don't Overuse Keywords:** If you use your keywords too often, you'll succeed in doing two things: first of all, you'll annoy the search engines and be accused of spamming. Second, you'll really annoy your readers, who you are hoping will become your customers. That's the last thing you want to do.

11. **Make Your Content Eye Catching:** Most people don't want to read paragraph after paragraph of "stuff." Break up your content with headlines, sub-headlines, bullet points, and lists. The easier you make your content to read, the more people will read it.

12. **Keep It Short:** Remember that eight-second attention span factoid from the beginning of this chapter? Keep that in mind when you are doing your writing. Blog posts should rarely, if ever, go more than 500 words. Any longer than that, and you risk losing your reader. And once they click away, chances are that they won't click back. So grab their attention in the beginning with a great headline, keep it with lists or bullet points, and get to your point quickly. Don't keep your readers waiting for what they need to find out.

13. **Write Like A Journalist:** Try to answer the five "W's" and "H" (who, what, when, where, why, and how) near the top of your content. This gives readers all the facts they need right away. Then, even if they choose not to read on, they'll have the most important information. If they have all this good stuff, it's a good bet that they will want to read on and find out more.

14. **Write Regularly:** Once you've started blogging, stick with it. Choose a schedule that feels comfortable to you, and stick to it. If your readers get used to hearing from you once a month, and then you disappear for a few months, you may not get those readers back.

15. **Always Include A Call To Action:** While you want your content to be informational, educational, and valuable, you still want your potential customers to know where and how they can find you. So all of your content should end with a call to action. Make it catchy and related to what you've written about, but be sure it includes your email address and/or phone number.

16. **Edit Your Work:** Or have someone do it for you. There's nothing that harms your credibility more quickly than copy that contains mistakes. The best way to edit your work is not to do it on your own at all but let someone else do it for you. Rest assured that another set of eyes would find a mistake or two that you missed. If that's not possible, try to give yourself some time away from the piece. Even if it's only an hour, once you come back to it with a clear head, you may see something you missed the first time. You can also try changing the font on your

computer and reread the work, or read it backwards. All of these things will help you find a misspelled word or missing period at the end of a sentence; they will hopefully help you avoid embarrassment once you've hit that "post" button.

17. **Don't Forget To Respond To Your Readers:** When readers leave a comment on a blog post or on your website, be sure to respond. Thank them for positive comments, and always respond politely. Above all else, don't respond negatively to a negative comment and start an online war of words. But don't ignore it either. If there's a negative comment on your post, reach out to the commenter offline to resolve the issue.

About Sue Toth

Sue Toth always had a devotion to the written word. The way written messages are presented–and received–is her passion. Sue wants to help you be sure your message is presented in the best light, so that your potential customers will read it and act on it.

In addition to helping you get your words out effectively, Sue will make sure they are polished, professional, and error-free. Not only is your message important, but the way it is presented is crucial as well. Errors harm your credibility, and Sue will work hard to make sure that errors don't happen.

Sue's experience with words spans more than two decades. She has worked as a reporter, feature writer, and editor. In addition to business writing, Sue is also an editor of fiction and nonfiction books, including romance, mystery, thriller, paranormal, and young adult. Nonfiction subjects include self-help, business, and politics. Sue also teaches writing at the college level, and has worked with undergraduate and graduate students at several colleges, including New York University, Fairleigh Dickinson University, Montclair State University, William Paterson University, and County College of Morris.

Contact Sue Today!

Website: http://www.editingbysue.com

Email: sue_toth@editingbysue.com

Phone: 973-362-5382

Facebook: http://facebook.com/editingbysue

Twitter: https://twitter.com/editingbysue

LinkedIn: https://www.linkedin.com/in/susanktoth

Chapter 8

Communicate Your Way to Success

Authored by Gloria Cirulli

A successful life can have many meanings to many people. For me, at the heart of it all is *effective* communication, which leads to not only making connections but truly *connecting* and *building* relationships with others. I suppose authenticity is an excellent descriptive for this; although some feel the word authenticity is overused, it is on the money when thinking about the depth and breadth of the relationships you form throughout your career of *not only business, but life.*

I learned this at a very early age from my parents. They both had an innate sense of making others feel welcome and cared for. And I feel blessed that both my sister and I inherited this trait. But in truth, it is much more than being born with the "caring gene." It is something that is taught and truly can be learned. Living in this environment gave me opportunities to observe and to participate in welcoming others into my life. This is when I also learned the value in people watching. I find this fascinating, and you can learn so much about someone by truly looking at them, their behaviors and how they interact with others. Growing up in this type of family started me on my journey of *genuinely* wanting to connect with others on a deeper level than just the surface. It was my introduction into *not* having the mind frame of "What's in it for me?" but rather, to explore relationships with others. When you approach situations like this, the gifts you give and receive abound! I am unbelievably fortunate to have some of the most incredible people in my life. And yes, on some level, I do believe, it has to do with some sort of law of attraction. Without ever consciously approaching life like this, it very often is a matter of what you give is what you get!

My life's journey, in general, has taken many twists and turns. I went from a career in the NYC sales promotion and advertising arena to moving to the burbs in New Jersey and becoming a small business owner with a brick and mortar location, to a stay-at-home mom, to a single parent who *needed* to go back to work, yet still *wanted* to be the team mom who baked the brownies and didn't miss *anything*! I would have had to become highly skilled in magic as well to master that. Short of becoming Samantha from "Bewitched" or Jeannie from "I Dream of Jeannie" I decided I would adapt how I was moving forward with my career and started a company with a business partner that could have an in-my-home office.

This was the time that it particularly struck a chord for me that building relationships was genuinely a two-way street. Being a working, single parent, the phrase, "It takes a village" rang true and took on a whole new meaning for me. I learned to ask my "village" that was our family support system to help be there for my children, as I was there for them in return. I knew this would help me to raise my sons in the manner in which I wanted, yielding the results that I wanted, having them thrive and grow into happy, well-adjusted and caring individuals. Very proudly, I can say that this has happened.

One of the mantras my sons heard over and over again in our home is, "Just because you hear someone's voice doesn't mean you are listening to what they are saying." I offer training programs for my clients to communicate more effectively with their clients, and people in general, by paying attention to what others are "saying." By listening to body language, words, even silence, you will rarely have to ask what they want or what they mean and to share freely and clearly what you want, as others are not mind readers. The importance of being engaged, not just engaging, and being interested, not just interesting is emphasized. Excelling at communicating is not only about being a good talker, it's about listening, observing, and expressing, too; and most importantly, combining and honing these skills. My clients have learned to connect with their prospects on a deeper level. This connection has increased their customer base and profits.

My career path has followed numerous directions over the years. As many of us have, I've changed industries, careers, been a multi-preneur© (an entrepreneur many times over and owned multiple businesses at the same time!) I've rebooted, revamped, segued, transitioned and even repositioned. At the core has always been that

I am a Powerhouse Communicator, and I utilize some of my best skills such as listening, creating, and sharing to somehow, and in some way, bring my clients' visions to life!

It has been a lesson well-learned that building strong, solid professional relationships is as important as building strong relationships in our personal lives with the "villages" we form. Whether you "play" in the corporate world, are an entrepreneur with a brick-and-mortar location, or you have a home-based office or are even in transition, it is crucial to find and build our tribe! Those we can call on for personal needs are very often not the same people we can call on for professional needs.

So how do we become part of a powerhouse tribe? It's not as tasking as it sounds. The key is to start by building quality relationships, surrounding ourselves with like-minded people, not necessarily exactly like ourselves, but with those who share the common goal of forming authentic relationships. Being part of organizations whose visions and philosophies resonate with your own is a great way to begin making the connections that lead to the relationships that build your tribe.

I am a people and business connector, *not* a business card collector! So when an opportunity presented itself to me to become a Managing Director for eWomenNetwork and build a Central NJ Chapter from scratch, it was a great fit. This has allowed me to utilize my expertise in networking by strategically connecting entrepreneurs and professionals through relationship building. We are an organization comprised of dynamic, action-oriented, like-minded individuals who genuinely and generously share resources, strategies, motivation and support to help one another grow and flourish both professionally and personally. It's *not* about shaking hands and exchanging business cards. It *is* about communicating and connecting! My clients call me the "Rock Star of Networking," because I offer strategies to have their networking work for them. One of the services I offer is to help my clients create their perfect elevator pitch, their ZIP™ (Zone In Please), so they can paint a picture with their words of who they are and what they offer! With a clear, concise message comes the opportunity to connect not only on a deeper level, but a broader one as well.

The phrase, "We do business with those we know, like and trust" is tried and true. No matter that we are in the age of advanced technology, this simply hasn't changed. I am passionate that effective communication leads to connecting, which is key to succeeding in business. This is how I've helped my clients turn their interactions into transactions!

As entrepreneurs and professionals, we often feel we need to convince others to get on board with what we are sharing. Whether making a sale to a client or motivating our team to get increased results. Getting others to listen and take action the way we would like them to can be a challenge. How many times have you thought, "I wish I knew what makes them tick" or "If only I could be a fly on the wall to hear their conversations?" or to possess the super power of reading minds! Then we would be able to dissuade any objections our customers have concerning purchasing and could get the outcome we want from our staff!

To achieve these results, we should be going about this from the opposite perspective. We tend to "talk the talk that we talk." So we need to stop talking "our language" and learn to speak to others the way they listen, sell to our customers the way they buy, and train our staff and team members the way that motivates them.

To effectively speak to all personality types is a skill that can be taught. I have programs for my clients to learn this in a quick, simple and scientifically-proven way. I offer the tools and training to customize your communication delivery for results-driven results: increased productivity, revenue, and motivation. Your message will come across clearly no matter what personality type you are speaking to, whether professionally, socially or personally. These skills are invaluable, and best of all they can be learned!

One of the best gifts you can give someone is to listen to them and make them feel you care. I carry this with me everywhere I go and is evident in not only my personal relationships, but my professional ones as well. I've learned over the years that most people just want their message to be heard and understood. It is extremely important how someone feels after your encounter with them is over. Do they feel you are genuine? Did you hear and understand their needs? Did they get the results they wanted? And in general, do they feel good about you and the situation? Ask yourself, if you were your client, would you want to do business with someone like you?

We all need to keep in mind that even if we don't consider ourselves to be sales people, we are all selling something, whether a product, service, concept, goal, vision or dream. But most importantly, we are selling ourselves. One of the greatest compliments I receive from my clients is when they share that they are "buying" me! This shows they have the faith and trust in me to deliver what they need to succeed!

A quote I feel applies to all aspects of life and is a favorite of mine is, "If you always do what you always did, you always get what you always got." Take inventory of the relationships in your life. Are they "working" the way they should and is the end result, the desired result? If not, then it is time to take the steps necessary to "Communicate Your Way To Success!"

About Gloria Cirulli

Gloria Cirulli is a Powerhouse Communicator! Her ZIP Technique can help you craft an attention grabbing elevator pitch! Her "Take STEPS to Success" Process will motivate you! As a Certified & Licensed Personality Assessment & Sales Trainer, Gloria offers the tools to sell to your customers the way they buy and train your team the way that motivates them. Gloria is the award winning Managing Director of eWomenNetwork Central NJ. As a connector, she is dedicated to bringing together entrepreneurs to share their expertise. Her monthly column for the Gannett syndication is featured in print and at myCentralJersey.com

Gloria lost over 100 pounds, 19 years ago and proudly raised two sons as a single mother. She has faced difficulties, yet stayed motivated to succeed! She is an engaging speaker and trainer! If you're ready to "Communicate Your Way to Success" connect with Gloria to schedule your complimentary phone Discovery Session.

Contact Gloria Today!

Website: http://www.gloriacirulli.com

Email: gloria@gloriacirulli.com

Phone: 732-266-3293

Crack Your Personality Code:
http://www.mybankcode.com/GloriaC

eWomenNetwork Central NJ:
http://www.eWomenNetwork.com/chapter/centralnj

Chapter 9

Delivering Outstanding Customer Service Drives Outstanding Financial Results

Authored by Gregory Stewart

All businesses from small, single-owner firms to the largest Fortune 500 firms need to review and measure their results. A business needs to understand their financial and operational performance and implement measurements to help them manage the business in an effective manner. An area that can be overlooked is customer service. The importance of why you should pay attention to this area is supported in a report from Forrester Research, which reveals that those organizations that best use customer data and analytics will have a major competitive edge. Here we will show you how your business can get moving forward, prepare for the future, and transform your culture to deliver outstanding results.

Transform your corporate culture

Developing a culture of delivering outstanding customer service can help you improve your results, gain a competitive edge, and drive your business forward. You need to develop the links between your organizational performance process and results with customer feedback so that you can validate you are supporting your customers. This can get overlooked because of the complexity of integrating your plans, processes, information, resource decisions, workforce capability & capacity, actions, results, and analysis to support key organization-wide goals that are the roadmap to your success. Financial management in your business is a critical tool for planning and directing the use of the company's resources. Profitability is the ability of a business to earn a profit. Profit is what remains of the revenue a business generates after it pays all expenses directly related to the generation of the revenue, such as producing a product and/or service, and other expenses related to the conduct of the business.

You cannot afford to forget that a major key to your success is your customers. They are your primary source for selling your product or service, and they are constantly being targeted by your competition. Customers who experience outstanding service tend to buy more often and do not negatively impact your support team to address service issues, saving you time and money!

If you develop a culture of outstanding customer service, you will help drive improved financial results. As a leader, you want all your employees to appreciate that one of the primary keys to success is your customers. They should be prepared to understand the company and be able to support all general customer business questions and be prepared to think beyond their job assignment and technical discipline and be able to interface directly with your customers, as needed, in support of their area of expertise.

To implement this change, a key area to focus on to help you achieve outstanding results is to track your customer's views on your service to them.

Measure results and customer satisfaction

Whether your business provides a service or manufactures a product, you need to develop a framework for measuring performance and planning in an uncertain business environment to help your business achieve and sustain the highest levels of profitability. Measurements should include:

- customer satisfaction and engagement
- product and service delivery, and process efficiency
- workforce satisfaction and engagement
- revenue and market share
- social responsibility

Superior Service

Everyone wants to pride themselves on their service, but that desire is often unsupported by the lack of timely measurements on what constitutes outstanding service. You need to demonstrate that your service is, indeed, worth paying for and be quick to react to customer service issues.

Develop a culture of outstanding customer service.

Key measurements to implement in your business:

1. Response time

2. Deadlines honored

3. Customers are the priority

4. Support functions are professional

5. Trust and candor

6. Respect for customer's culture and operation

7. Speed of response

   a) are you proactive?

   b) do you follow-up?

   c) do you check-in on occasion with your customers?

How do you drive this change in focus? Leaders set the direction and tone for the organization. You as the leader need to establish customer service as a cornerstone of your culture. You can set the tone right from the start, by being a participant in new-employee orientations, organizational meetings, and town hall meetings. The leaders must emphasize the importance of delivering superior customer service by everyone, at all levels of the organization.

Superior service is a key differentiator, and because it requires no major capital investment it is often easier than other company changes. Our focus is on seven key measurements. However, your business may require service level measurements that exceed the seven key measurements on which we work with our customers. Adding measurements is not an issue. However, it is critical that you are able to articulate them and extend them to your organization and customers.

Implementing Customer service measurements

Why do you want to implement service measurements and develop a company culture that will focus on your customers? High service levels always assist the perception of value, so they need to be a cornerstone from the first point of introduction to a prospective client to your most seasoned customer.

An example of why this investment in service can help your business is found in a retail dry cleaning service in New Jersey. A customer had come in to complain about the quality of their garment. The counter clerk started to resist, but the owner interrupted and overruled the clerk. When the customer returned, he was provided with a check to replace the garment. The owner took action and reviewed the importance with the team of delivering outstanding customer service, and that this is a key requirement for their employment. Later that day, the customer returned with a few friends whom he had shared his experience. The direct result was a dramatic increase in dry cleaning business, because this customer was happy and shared the news about how customer-centric they were with his friends and neighbors.

To get started you need to develop a culture with some key measurements:

1. **Response time.**

   Return call-backs at a minimum the same day they were made (or first thing the next morning, if they called late in the afternoon). Strive to return calls within a few hours. Email responses should always occur within 24 hours.

2. **Deadlines honored.**

   Reports, responses, and anything else requested would be delivered in worst case on deadline and, in best case, considerably before it. This includes last-minute requests and short-deadline request. A customer should never have to follow-up with your firm to obtain an awaited document or e-mail.

3. **The customer is the priority.**

You and your team do not take customer calls on a cell phone forwarded to you while you're in transit or, worst case, working with another client. Never make a customer feel rushed, taken for granted or patronized. Your organizations must provide their undivided attention. Every customer knows you can't be available every time they call, but they should expect that when you do connect they will not be competing for your focus.

4. **Your support functions are professional.**

If a customer talks to your assistant, answering service, or even voice mail, the team needs to treat them with respect. The customer should never have to "jump through hoops." Do not make them listen to the same 30-second commercial for your services every time they call simply to leave you a message. All letters and email need to be error-free and, electronically, it needs to be compatible with the customer's electronic platforms and applications.

5. **Perceive trust and candor.**

   Do not have your team extend or contribute to the problem! You need to candidly inform your customers when something has gone wrong. This can also include an honest discussion with your team about their unprofessional behavior if that has become an issue.

6. **Respect your customer's culture and operation.** After you have taken the time to learn about how your customer operates, don't make unreasonable demands and commit silly mistakes. Your teams should proactively pay for expenses like coffee, park in the correct area, observe office policies, and request expense reimbursement commensurate with the situation (e.g., if your team flies coach and takes taxis, that's the level of reimbursement you request).

7. **Be proactive.**

   Periodically share articles, ideas, references, and other resources that are non-promotional and clearly helpful to the company, position, and/or life. You should provide more than expected and anticipate what the customer is in need of to ensure that their needs are exceeded, not merely met.

A successful business leader has clearly defined core values and measurements. A key is leading all the components of your organization to achieve your mission, ongoing success, and performance excellence. Make customer service your secret weapon for business and financial success. You can develop a culture of outstanding customer support as your competitive edge in the marketplace to differentiate yourself from your competitor. A "happy" customer is your goal; they normally pay sooner, recommend your business, and are more likely to buy again. Delivering outstanding customer service will help you grow your business and deliver outstanding financial results.

About Gregory (Greg) W. Stewart

Greg is a hands-on Business Adviser and Executive Coach who works with business owners to help them attain the goals and objectives of their business so they can manage the business and not have it manage them.

Greg specializes in delivering Breakthrough RESULTS with entrepreneurs, business owners, and managers who are frustrated with the performance and operation of their business.

Although Greg works with businesses of all sizes, most of his clients are start-ups that are not achieving their business plan outlook, and more established firms that are not achieving their historical results and have stopped growing. The focus is to identify what issues are holding the business back, prioritize them, and modify them within their budget. These efforts continue to deliver improved profitability, employee satisfaction, and a successful business.

Are you ready to take control of your business and start achieve the Breakthrough RESULTS! you need and want?

Contact Greg Today!

Website: http://www.NexGenMgt.com

Email: gwstewart@NexGenMgt.com

LinkedIn: https://www.linkedin.com/in/gregorywstewart

Facebook: https://www.facebook.com/NexGenMgt/

Chapter 10

Communicate to Win

Authored by Jill Vitiello

Jeanne walked out of the CEO's office in a daze. Tom had just reviewed the results of the annual employee opinion survey with her. Scores had plummeted, and verbatim comments were harsh. Employees reported low morale as well as distrust of Jeanne and her senior leadership team. As the Chief Information Officer responsible for an Information Technology organization of hundreds of professionals whose responsibilities impacted every corner of the company, this was bad news for Jeanne. Her department was leading a systems upgrade that was the first phase of a company-wide reengineering initiative, which was critical to improving the company's profitability. And, employee buy-in was essential to its success.

As she made her way back to her office, Jeanne reflected on the past year and tried to make sense of the survey findings. Yes, the transformation had been a struggle, and people, herself included, were working harder than ever. Jeanne had heard some grumbling here and there, but she hadn't let it take her focus off the project. Besides, she supported communications within the IT department. There was the newsletter that her admin sent out now and then and the occasional online chats that she led. Jeanne had even spent a day last month visiting the Midwest region. What did employees expect?

What do Employees Want?

If you are a business leader like Jeanne, it's likely you know exactly how she feels. Have you been blindsided by the results of your organization's employee opinion survey? Has your boss held you accountable for improving morale, or else? It's possible you are just as baffled as Jeanne. In spite of your best efforts to provide employees with the information and tools they need to do their jobs, they never seem satisfied. What more do they want?

Jeanne knew she had to turn the situation around in a hurry. And, the only way to do that was to get employees engaged. Experts define "employee engagement" as people's willingness to expend discretionary effort, in other words, do more than what is expected of them as outlined in their job descriptions. People are more likely to be engaged when their opinions and expertise are considered in decision making and when their contributions are recognized as worthwhile by managers they respect.

The benefits of an engaged workforce are widely recognized. Researchers have found that companies with the highest level of growth in profitability (about 10-15%) occurred in companies whose employees were described as "highly engaged." Conversely, disengaged employees are estimated to cost U.S. companies between $450 billion to $550 billion, according to a Gallup poll. Leaders who dismiss employee engagement as a "soft" issue that can be left to the Human Resources department do so at their own peril.

Communicate to Win: The RACE Model

Working with Vitiello Communications Group (VTLO), Jeanne and her senior leadership team used our RACE model to get to the heart of the matter. The IT executives recognized that to achieve the department's goals, they needed to foster genuine engagement, not just raise survey scores. They realized that their people wanted to do meaningful work that was valued by leaders they trusted. But, where to start?

VTLO partnered with the team to introduce our four-step RACE model, which is an acronym for Research, Action, Communicate and Evaluate. Here's a brief overview of how it works:

Research

- Start with data. Like Jeanne, use the results of your employee opinion survey as a baseline. Compare your team's results with other teams across the organization.

- Interview key stakeholders inside and outside the organization. Find out how employees' attitudes are impacting co-workers as well as suppliers and customers.

- Conduct focus groups to give employees a forum for voicing their opinions. Prompt discussion; listen as they identify the problems and suggest solutions.

- Perform a communications audit to evaluate how people receive, send and process information.

Action

- Benchmark your findings against best practices and industry standards.

- Brainstorm potential solutions with a small, diverse group of employees.

- Create a Findings and Recommendations Report. Socialize the recommendations with senior leaders and a sampling of front-line supervisors, customer-facing employees and stakeholders outside the department.

- Test which recommendations are likely to succeed in your workplace culture.

Communicate

- Plan ahead. Based on the feedback you received, draft a communications plan that spans 12 months. The plan should include: audiences you intend to reach, strategic messages that will guide your communications, and the communications channels you plan to use. Be creative so you can capture your employees' attention.

- Prepare to launch the communications plan by enrolling managers and supervisors, informing them of desired outcomes, showing them how they can participate, and providing the tools needed to get started.

- Promote your new approach to communication and engagement by announcing the program, letting all employees know what to expect, and delivering on that promise throughout the year.

Evaluate

- Define what success looks like for your organization. Leaders who communicate to win know the goal of the activities, and, therefore, can assess the return on investment.

- Evaluate your plan as it unfolds. Don't wait for the annual employee opinion survey to find out how employees are responding to your communications and engagement plan. Use simple, fast techniques to measure progress such as online metrics and pulse check meetings; then adjust your plan as needed.

VTLO's RACE Model

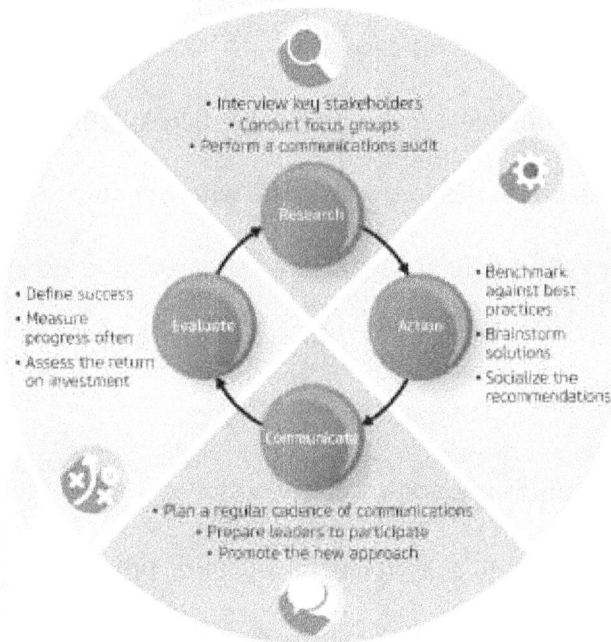

A Caveat: RACE, Don't Speed

Like many leaders, Jeanne was eager to see results and was tempted to jump to tactics. By listening to her employees, however, she learned which communication channels they preferred and what messages resonated with them. She invested the time to create a plan that ensured a regular cadence of communication. As you consider the RACE model for your own use, focus first on the small, simple changes you can make immediately to engage employees. Write those actions into the first 90 days of your plan.

Winning over the Workforce

Jeanne had the courage to make significant changes in the way she and her senior leaders interacted with employees. Instead of pushing out information haphazardly, they committed themselves to sustaining a dialog with employees through digital and in-person communications. Their new plan included:

- **Online communication** – The newsletter was repurposed as an online community with content that is refreshed weekly. A biweekly email to all employees summarizes the news and provides quick links back to the site. Employees can like, share, comment and vote on content as well as contribute original content to the community.

- **Face-to-face recognition** – Once yearly formal town hall meetings were replaced with monthly "birthday breakfasts" with

Jeanne and senior leadership team members. The leaders enjoy breakfast with employees whose birthday falls in that particular month, then provide a brief update on the state of the business and the department, and hold an informal Q&A.

- **Employee ambassadors** – A department-wide campaign invited IT employees to volunteer for the newly formed ambassador council. Members are responsible for identifying newsworthy success stories to publish on the online community, and for raising employees' concerns to the senior leadership team.

Six months later, the company took the unprecedented action of administering the employee opinion survey off-cycle. Shortly afterward, Tom called Jeanne into his office – this time to ask her to explain the amazing turnaround. The IT department's scores had improved significantly – up more than 20 percentage points. Verbatim comments complimented the CIO and her senior leaders for listening and taking appropriate action. The company-wide system integration was going smoothly, and profitability was up. Tom was so impressed that he asked Jeanne to share her approach with her peers on the executive committee to align the entire company for improved employee engagement.

Call to Action

When Jeanne called to share this wonderful news, she told me that, through her work with us, she had learned that a leader's most important job is to engage her people. By including employees in the communication process, she won them over and inspired them to action and success. Jeanne had learned how to communicate to win.

Jeanne is one of many business leaders we work with who communicate to win using our proven approach. If you are reading this book, you are a winner interested in breakthrough results. Whether your office is in the C-suite or on Main Street, you can leverage the power of language to drive the business results and the breakthrough you desire.

For a free, no-obligation phone consultation to put you on the path to achieving breakthrough results through effective communication, please call 732-238-6622 to make your appointment with me, Jill Vitiello, president, Vitiello

Communications Group. Contact info@vtlo.com for more information.

Still not sure your communications need to breakthrough? I invite you to take our nine-question true/false online survey. In just a couple of minutes, you'll get an instant read on the vital signs of your company's communications.

We welcome a dialog with you!

About Jill Vitiello

Jill Vitiello is the founder and president of Vitiello Communications Group (VTLO), a creative agency focused on helping leaders communicate to win. As the go-to expert for employee engagement, leadership and change communication, VTLO leverages the power of language to drive business results. The company provides communications services for leaders at Fortune 500 and other influential companies in industries such as pharmaceuticals, financial services and manufacturing.

As a recognized communications industry leader, Jill has served as an officer on multiple industry association boards and is passionate about business communications, entrepreneurship and empowering women.

Leaders who work with VTLO see significant spikes in employee satisfaction scores and experience engagement that exceeds expectations. Are you interested in communications that help you achieve your breakthrough results? I invite you to get to know me and my team of consultants by scheduling a free, no obligation phone consultation.

Contact Jill and VTLO Today!

Website: http://www.vtlo.com

Email: info@vtlo.com

Phone: 732-238-6622

Twitter: @JillVitiello, @VTLOcomms

LinkedIn: http://linkedin.com/in/jillvitiello

Chapter 11

Getting HR Right – Knowing Your Culture

Authored by Laura Crothers Osborn

How would you describe your organizations' culture?

Culture is something you feel. When it's good it keeps the team together, motivated and moving toward a common goal. When it's not on the radar, and just happens, it can result in the opposite. If it's not discussed, planned or aligned it can slowly decay, creating retention and engagement problems, or even ethical concerns. These things can cost a company and its' owners Time, Energy and Money.

Time, Energy and Money that you would rather be spending

growing your business, or delighting your clients. Deliberately creating the culture and the people who represent you is one key to achieving breakthrough results.

Over the years, many of my clients hit their growth stride and engage me to help with some part of the Human Resource (HR) process – setting up a recruitment strategy and process, designing a compensation framework or plan, coaching new managers or current leaders, creating on-boarding processes, designing or fixing something quickly.

I start each project by understanding not only the business growth plan but the culture you are trying to create. Aligning HR Practices to those two things has been a huge differentiator for my successful clients.

Right now, you may be wondering - what do HR practices have to do with culture? Let me tell you about a company I worked with: *The CEO understood the power of culture. They were a high growth, private equity backed, start-up organization, who grew quickly to 150 employees and became an industry leader. That was their goal and I built HR practices to support it. Employee voluntary turnover rate was < 5%, employee and customer satisfaction rates* *were both > 90% - they had created a place people loved.*

How did they differ from other high growth organizations I have been involved with? **We spent hours discussing culture regularly.**

They were able to articulate what they wanted the company to feel like to employees and customers, things like:

- *The anti-beaurocracy*
- *Fast paced and high performing*
- *Client service oriented – including being flexible*
- *Collaborative with that entrepreneurial feeling - employees feel they were personally contributing to creating something special*
- *Fun and friendly*
- *Attract the very best people. People with character and passion, who were known for getting things done, well liked "Real People"*

Outlined in this chapter are six (6) areas of discussion including questions I pose to my clients as we think about aligning HR practices with culture. Thinking through these will help propel you toward your breakthrough results. *I will illustrate the impact by applying it to the high growth company I mentioned above.*

SOURCING

Where are you going to find prospective employees? Specifically, what companies would you like to target? *In my example, they wanted people in their industry known for being the best at what they do – mostly from large national firms.*

How are you going to attract these employees? *We had to think about how to attract employees from large well known organizations to come join a start-up. One main differentiator would be the culture.*

COMPENSATION AND BENEFITS

What do you need to pay them? What should the total compensation be? What type of split between base and variable pay?

As a start-up and keeping in line with the entrepreneurial ownership culture - we put more at risk, allowing for higher rewards opportunities and lower fixed costs. I created compensation plans to allow everyone to share in the success of the business and sales plans that had no caps -- "you eat what you kill". Top sales people wanted to work there because they were paid well, and they were confident they'd bring the business. Marginal sales people didn't last. That was the high performance culture.

How do you want to design jobs? You may want to think outside of the traditional box. *We designed jobs to be more end to end, instead of silos of repetitive tasks, this helped attract people who wanted a new challenge and were passionate about their work and wanted to create something with the knowledge they brought to the table.*

What type of benefits do you need to offer? I recommend thinking about designing one benefit that you can really talk about. *Benefits needed to be somewhat competitive, but within a start-up budget. Vacation time started at 4 weeks – that was something no one else was doing for new hires.*

RECRUITMENT

See how these pieces play into creating a recruitment strategy!

What do you show or tell candidates upfront to attract them?

How would you explain your culture and why you are different? What is your sourcing strategy? What is your interview process?

TIP: One recruiting strategy that many clients implement is an Employee Referral Program. They are an easy, effective and inexpensive way to recruit qualified talent. Employees already understand the culture, so they do the selling and recruiting to the people they like and trust. *Over 75% of people hired the first two years were Employee Referrals...* Employee Referral Programs clearly save Time, Energy and Money.

GOLDEN RULE: Hire Slow, Fire Fast. Take your time, involve a few people in the interview process, and make sure you get a good feel for the candidate and how they would fit into the culture. Ask open ended questions and let them do most of the talking. If you are unsure, bring them back in – then TRUST YOUR GUT. If you decide you made a hiring mistake, address the performance concerns early on and act decisively.

RETENTION

What are you going to do to retain your employees once you have hired them? Are there development opportunities? What is the philosophy on performance management and who owns it – the employee, the manager or HR? How can you engage people with one another in a collaborative way, to create lasting friendships, to make their time at work pleasurable?

The example company was being deliberate and intentional about behaving differently from the large competitors. Monthly fun included things like Pina Coladas for summer, playing instruments in the office, philanthropic activities voted on by the employees. The executives delivered ice cream, flipped burgers, played games, and sent notes of thanks. Access to leaders was part of the appeal and kept the culture anti-beaurocratic and fun.

Retention is one way to measure the effectiveness of the culture created. Annual engagement surveys are another way to ensure ongoing effectiveness.

EXITS

How will you exit people? This includes those who select to leave for a new opportunity, as well as, those who aren't working out because their skills don't match when the company grows and the jobs evolve. (Not because of ethical or attendance issues). What do you want to learn from an exit interview?

How you exit an employee impacts not only that person, but also the remaining employees. Many of our clients have created an Alumni Network of ex-employees, who can become future clients, referral sources or even re-hires. I believe strongly in treating people the right way, which isn't necessarily following a 10 step disciplinary process.

In our example, given the fast paced culture, it was important to have meaningful regular on-going feedback. Being the anti-beaurocracy, HR tried to allow the person a role in the discussion and the decision to exit. They let them exit gracefully. People had transition time, were offered lower levels jobs where appropriate, were not pariah.

GOLDEN RULE: Always treat people with dignity and respect. Even in exiting people, you should align practice to culture. It's a strong statement.

LEADERSHIP

Finally and most importantly, how do your leaders affect the culture of the organization? Are they self-aware of their impact?

Are they a high performing team, supporting and trusting each other? Do you have a strong bench?

I believe Leadership Development should be a conscious decision as a business enabler to support your culture. *Working with the best 360 tool in the world, The Leadership Circle ™, leaders gained insight into their leadership effectiveness by getting feedback from their boss, peers, subordinates and clients. That was compared to normative data of tens of thousands of leaders. This tool also assesses the impact of the collective leadership on culture.*

Awareness is the start of the journey.

Then second level managers were assessed – the people who had to turn the leadership ideas into action all while continuing to be aware of their individual and collective impact on culture. It was very powerful for the CEO to see the data for these two groups and create a roadmap for development spend of Time, Energy and Money.

These six HR areas should may help you uncover any gaps you have in realizing your culture.

We as leaders need to be thoughtful about the Culture we are creating and the People we are asking to join us on our journey. We need to create the vision, lay out the culture and make sure our practices are aligned to enable our employees to create Breakthrough Results for our clients.

About Laura Crothers Osborn

Laura Crothers Osborn leads Crothers HR Consulting, LLC a highly successful Human Resource consulting firm founded in 2010. They provide coaching and HR guidance to leaders determining the best ways to attract, integrate, engage and retain their human capital talent. Her clients include high growth small and middle market private and public businesses. She is known for designing HR practices in a way that align with culture, and create working environments marked by authenticity and creative action rather than caution and fear.

Before starting her practice, Laura held the position of Chief People Officer of EverBank Commercial Finance, where she created and staffed the HR function in two predecessor start-up organizations. She understands the need to be nimble and react quickly to changing dynamics while growing an organization from eight to 250 employees in five years.

Through her years in Human Resource leadership roles in organizations such as McGraw-Hill, Merrill Lynch, CIT, ADP and Shearson Lehman Brothers she lead and/or facilitated many initiatives focused on compensation design, integration, leadership training and coaching, change management, performance management as well as employee relations. Her breadth of experiences includes the unique technical role of Senior Director; HR focused on Mergers and Acquisitions at Standard & Poor's leading HR due diligence and integration planning and execution.

Laura lives with her husband and their two boys in New Jersey. She spends much of her time on the sidelines of football, lacrosse or baseball fields, and spends winter weekends skiing at Windham Mountain.

Contact Laura Today!

Website: http://www.CrothersHRConsulting.com

Email: Laura@CrothersHRConsulting.com

LinkedIn: https://www.linkedin.com/in/laura-crothers-osborn-043255b

Chapter 12

Protect Your Hearth, Home and Business

Authored by Anne Thornton

Owning a home or commercial property is a major responsibility. In my 25 years of owning a property management and plumbing/remodeling contracting company, I have seen almost everything go wrong in a house or commercial building. Why? Usually, it's because owners either ignore what is happening for too long, or they just don't know how to evaluate the physical property. To protect your property and maintain or enhance its property value, pay attention to these ten tips, tricks, and techniques, and you will have a much better outcome.

Please note: All of the information regarding codes, permits, and other construction laws are accurate for New Jersey. If you reside somewhere else other than New Jersey, please check the requirements of your particular state and local code officials.

1. **When work is needed, hire a professional contractor.**

Most people's first inclination is to pay the least amount for a property or home repair. But the adage is true in this case – you get what you pay for – and the consequences can be a very big deal. If you do go the route of the carpenter in a pickup truck with a magnetic sign and a dog riding shotgun, with no insurance, don't give him too much money up front.

You are better off to seek out a local professional who is experienced in the latest building products and technology, assuring you the highest quality job. If the trade is licensed, i.e. electrician, plumber, home inspector, pest control, etc., ask for a copy of his or her license, and you can verify with the appropriate state agency. Many licensed trades also have industry certifications; you should ask for copies of those and make verifications. A professional's knowledge and experience can save you time, money and aggravation.

Professionals are familiar with local building codes and regulations. You can be assured that the project will be built right. Permits are required for many home repairs:

- Water heater replacement; electric and plumbing permits are required.

- Chimney (flue) certification may also be required if gas water heater.

- Bonding wires between hot and cold water required.

- Any addition of electrical outlets or circuits requires a permit.

- Smoke detectors and carbon monoxide detectors are always required. However, they may be subject to verification when inspectors inspect for any permit items.

- Heating or air conditioning equipment replacement; electric and plumbing permits required.

- Fire and Chimney (flue) permits may also be required.

State law requires that contractors must be insured. Ask for an insurance certificate. Make sure the contractor has liability, business and workers compensation insurance. Ask your insurance agent to review any certificates if you are unsure how to read them. Accidental damage can happen to anyone, but only a professional is insured for such mishaps.

A professional contractor is solvent with a line of credit. You will not be required to pay in full until your project is completed. Also, professional contractors know when and when NOT to charge sales tax. Some heating items and some capital improvements do not require sales tax but do require certain forms to be filled out for the appropriate state agencies.

Ask for references. Like any professional, a builder or plumber is proud of his/her work. Some states require that contractors be registered as a Home Improvement Contractor. Ask for a copy of their license. Licenses, certifications, registrations, insurance, permits are for you and your neighbors' protection! Don't take short cuts to save a couple of dollars, it could cost you thousands.

2. Check your fire and carbon monoxide alarms.

Make sure you have enough and that they are working. You want to test them periodically and make sure that they can be heard in all parts of your house. Push and hold the test button for a few seconds. The detector should produce a loud noise. To test whether the unit will work in a fire, you can purchase a small spray can of "smoke detector test aerosol" at most hardware stores. Follow the directions. If your alarm does not go off, even if it beeps when you hold the button down, it is a non-functioning fire alarm. Try changing the batteries and cleaning the detector to remove any dust, and then repeat the procedure. If it doesn't work again, replace the unit as soon as possible

3. Clogged dryer vents cause fires!

More than 15,000 dryer vent fires occur every year in the United States, according to the U.S. Consumer Product Safety Commission. Dryer vent fires are a real problem in newer, bigger homes where the dryer is placed in the center of the house and not up against an outside wall. Some of these dryer vents can run 15, 20, 25 feet to exhaust to the outside. That's a lot of length with twists and turns.

Here are some of the signs that it's time to clean your vent: Clothes are not completely dry after a normal drying cycle, and it takes longer than 35-40 minutes to dry a load. You smell a musty odor in the clothing after the drying cycle. Clothing seems unusually hot to the touch after a complete drying cycle. The dryer vent hood flap does not properly open as it is designed to do during the operation of the dryer. Debris is noticed within the outside dryer vent opening. Excessive heat is noticed within the room in which the dryer is being operated. Large amounts of lint accumulate in the lint trap during operation. A visible sign of lint and debris is noticed around the lint filter. An excessive odor is noticed from dryer sheets that are used during the drying cycle.

4. Pay attention to your furnace and air conditioning units.

Every fall and spring, have a professional heating/air conditioning contractor inspect and maintain your systems as recommended by the manufacturer. Maintenance should include: cleaning, lubricating fans and motors, tightening or changing belts, checking electrical safeties, drain pan for leaks, condensation drain, testing the capacitors, calibrating the thermostat. Here are also some things you can maintain throughout the year and save money: change your AC filter at least every three months (or more depending on how heavily you are using your air conditioner), consider having your ducts cleaned by a professional cleaning company, check the condensate hose to be sure it is not blocked with algae, clean the outside condensing unit screen of leaves, and always listen for unusual noises. If you are unsure, ask your contractor to show you how to perform these maintenance items.

5. Know how to turn off the water to your house.

If you suffer a major leak of any kind in your home, you may need to turn the water off to the entire house. Learn how to do it and teach everyone who lives in your house how to do it. If you have a water emergency, you will be glad you did.

6. If your washing machine hoses burst, it's a big, big deal.

If your washing machine hoses burst, the water will constantly run. That means water will flow out at about 650 gallons per hour flooding everything. Here are a few things you can do to prevent that from happening in your home.

- Turn off the washing machine valve after every use.

- Never leave a washing machine going if you are not home.

- Check the condition of the hoses to make sure there are no kinks.

- Install 20-year guaranteed Floodchek washing machine hoses (only available online at http://www.floodchek.com).

7. Water heaters need tender loving care, too.

The water heater is something most of us take for granted until it suddenly stops working. Water heater maintenance is easy to overlook, because the tank just sits there and has no moving parts to worry about. But inside, two things are constantly attacking your water heater: **sediment and rust**. To keep your water heater operating correctly, and to extend its life by years, your water heater needs regular maintenance to minimize rust and calcium carbonate. This should be done by an experienced and licensed plumber. However, there is one easy thing that you can do throughout the year, and that is to check around the base of your water heater for evidence of leaks. If your water heater is over five years old, it should be checked monthly for any leakage or rusting at the bottom. If water leakage or rust is found, the water heater should be replaced. Regular annual maintenance will definitely enhance the operation of your water heater, save you money and saves in your general energy consumption.

8. Preventing water damage is a big deal.

There are many ways to prevent leaks and water intrusion in your home or commercial property. The following list will help you identify areas to look at on a regular basis to make sure everything remains in good condition.

Flashing: Flashing is a thin metal strip found around doors, windows, thresholds, chimneys, and roofs, and is designed to prevent water from getting into spaces where two different building surfaces meet.

Vents: All vents, including clothes dryers, gable vents, attic vents, and exhaust vents, should have hood exhaust to the exterior, be in good working order, and have boots.

Attics: Check for holes, air leaks, or bypasses from the house, and make sure there is enough insulation to keep the heat from the house from escaping. Any air leak or inadequate insulation can result in ice damming. To look for leaks, check the bottom side of the roof sheathing and roof rafters/trusses for water stains.

Basements: Make sure that basement windows and doors have built-up barriers around them. Inspect your sump pump to ensure it is working properly (a battery backup system is recommended for sump pumps). The sump pump should discharge as far away from the house as possible.

Humidity: The relative humidity in your home should be between 30% and 50%. When you see condensation on windows or wet stains on walls and ceilings or have musty smells, these are all signs that you have too much humidity in your home. Stagnant air is humidity's best friend; so check all the areas in your home where air does not circulate – places like behind curtains, under beds, and in closets. You are looking for dampness and mildew. Tell your family when taking showers or baths, they should always use the exhaust fan to help move the humid air out of the room. Never turn the air conditioner off when you leave on a trip; only turn it up. Your air conditioning system helps remove moisture from your home. If you are concerned at all about the humidity level in your home, consult with a mechanical contractor or air conditioning repair company to determine if your HVAC system is properly sized and in good working order.

Air Conditioners: Every air conditioner unit should have a drain pan. Take a look at your pan to make sure it is draining freely, has no standing water, and is adequately sloped toward the outlets. Of course, make sure drain lines are clean and clear of any obstruction.

Drywall: Drywall is an extremely porous material and is difficult to dry out completely. If you see signs of moisture on any drywall, those damaged areas should be cut out and replaced.

Expansion Joints: Expansion joints absorb movement and are the materials between bricks, pipes, and other building materials. If expansion joints are not in good condition, water can infiltrate. Take a look at any expansion joints on your property regularly and if there are cracks in the joint sealant, remove the old sealant, install a backer rod and fill with a new sealant.

Exterior Wood Sheathing and Siding: Replace any wood siding and sheathing that appears to have water damage. The exterior wood sided wall should have at least eight inches between the wood and the earth.

Landscaping: Keep trees trimmed so that branches are at least 7 feet away from any exterior house surface. This will help prolong the life of your siding and roof and prevent insects from entering your home from the tree. Vines should be kept off all exterior walls because they can help open cracks in the siding, which allows moisture or insects to enter the house.

Irrigation: Inspect and adjust the spray pattern of the irrigation heads to minimize the water sprayed directly onto the house to avoid excessive water near the foundation.

Windows and Doors: Check for leaks around your windows and doors, especially near the corners. Check for peeling paint because it can be a sign of water getting into the wood. Look for discolorations in paint or caulking and swelling of the window or door frame or surrounding materials.

Roof: Repair or replace shingles around any area that allows water to penetrate the roof sheathing. The most common leaks are around chimneys, plumbing vents, and attic vents. Roof leaks can be hard to trace because the water may run along the attic floor, rafters, or truss for quite a distance before coming through the ceiling.

Foundation and Exterior Walls: Seal any cracks and holes in external walls, joints, and foundations. In particular, examine locations where piping or wiring extends through the outside walls. Fill all cracks in these locations with sealant.

Plumbing: Check for leaking faucets, dripping or "sweating" pipes, clogged drains, and faulty water drainage systems. Inspect washing machine hoses and water heaters too.

Termite-Damaged Material: Check for termite damage in wood materials such as walls, beams, or floors. Any wood exposed to the exterior can potentially lead to moisture intrusion or termite infestation.

9. Don't forget your appliances!

Whether it is in your home or your office kitchenette, appliances get used a lot. Here are some tips to keep those appliances in good working order.

- Vacuum the coils behind the refrigerator. Cleaning the coils regularly help the refrigerator to run more efficiently, extending the life of the unit.

- For the dishwasher, the spray arm, air gap, and strainer should regularly be cleaned.

- The easiest way to clean a garbage disposal is to fill up the sink with two to four inches of hot, soapy water. By pulling the plug and running the garbage disposal, hot, soapy water will be pulled through cleaning as it goes.

10. Seasonal duties to be performed.

- Always have a multi-purpose fire extinguisher accessible. Check it annually to make sure it is in good working condition.

- Remove screens from windows and install storm windows (helps reduce the cost to heat your home and prevents window sills from rotting).

- Clean out gutters and downspouts (helps keeps ice dams from forming).

- Insulate pipes in your home's crawl spaces and attic (keeps pipes from freezing – the more insulation, the better!).

- Store firewood at least 30 feet away from your home (reduces the chance of fire and termites).

- Familiarize responsible family members with the gas main valve and other appliance valves (if you are not sure, have a plumber come out to teach you).

- Make sure all electrical holiday decorations have tight connections (Use three-prong plugs and cords for best grounding, and unplug when not in use. Cords should never be bundled together or run under rugs or carpet).

- Check the attic for adequate ventilation (check the exterior wall to be sure ceiling insulation is not blocking outside air from soffit vents).

- Clean the kitchen exhaust hood and air filter (keeping the hood clean of cooking grease helps keep a stove-top fire from spreading).

- Check the water hoses on the clothes washer, refrigerator ice maker and dishwasher for cracks and bubbles (replace any hoses that show signs of leaking).

- Test all ground-fault-circuit-interrupter (GFCI) outlets (these should be tripped and reset once a month; if they do not trip or reset, have the outlet changed by a qualified electrician).

You can really save money and aggravation if you practice these 10 tips, tricks and techniques to protect your investment in your home and business! Pass on this great information to your family, neighbors and colleagues too.

About Anne Thornton

Anne owns and runs one of New Jersey's few woman owned plumbing and remodeling companies. MSI Plumbing & Remodeling has been providing plumbing, remodeling and building repair services for residential and commercial properties for over 25 years.

Services include remodeling of kitchens, bathrooms & basements. Plus all licensed plumbing services including servicing and repairing fixtures and faucets, standard and high-efficiency water heaters, well tanks, water conditioning systems, gas lines inside and outside of the home and any plumbing re-pipe.

Contact Anne today!

Website: http://www.MSIPlumbingandRemodeling.com/

Email: Anne@MSIPlumbingandRemodeling.com

Chapter 13

Concussion: Breaking Through the Misconceptions

Authored by Kristine C. Keane, Psy.D.

There are many ways to achieve better, breakthrough results in business ranging from clever marketing, team building, and discipline. However, at the end of any given day, true success becomes less about how many deadlines you conquered or numbers you've made and is clearly about what you have contributed to the lives of other people. Success is about helping others become better versions of themselves. The rest, the goal obtaining, the numbers, the achievements, (or, however we define our success), seems to follow naturally after we have understood this principle of success.

As a neuropsychologist, over the past 15 years, I have treated numbers of children and adults who have sustained concussions as a result of sports, recreation, falls or accidents. However, concussion is, and has been over the past 5 or so years, a shiny, new and hot topic in the news, popular media, and in sports. Since 2009, the media has exploded with news about our beloved athletes who have sustained concussions and continue to suffer from cognitive and physical deficits years after the game. The media has also burst with stories about new gadgets and preventative gear, such as new helmets, soccer headbands, and dental appliances, all of which promise to lower the risk of or eliminate a concussion. Concussion has become so widely popularized and talked about. There has also been a surge of phone apps, inclusion in video games and more recently, a major motion picture.

Although, the attention that concussion has gotten has its pros and cons, and is not without controversy. On the one hand, the more attention the topic of concussion has received, the more research and valid information is available to people to prevent and treat concussions safely. On the other hand, there remains a lot of misinformation available due to wide variation in physician knowledge, media miscoverage, and financial gains made by gear and treatments. There is great controversy about making rule changes in sports, and which rule changes effectively keep players safer. There is even greater controversy about what exactly constitutes a subconcussive blow, and what constitutes too many concussions. At what point should we call it quits?

In my neuropsychology practice, since we cannot ultimately stop a concussion from happening, we define our success by how effective we have been in educating our patients and our community about how to prevent head injury, how to become aware of the injury and how to properly manage a concussion. "As the ability to treat or reduce the effects of concussive injury after the event is minimal, education of athletes, colleagues, and the general public is a mainstay of progress in this field. Athletes, referees, administrators, parents, coaches, and healthcare providers must be educated regarding the detection of concussion, its clinical features, assessment techniques and principles of safe RTP." Zurich Statement, 2014.

What is concussion? The American College of Rehabilitation Medicine's often cited definition of concussion is "a physiological disruption of brain function as a result of a traumatic event as manifested by at least one of the following: alteration in mental state, loss of consciousness, focal neurological deficit, that may or may not be transient, but where the severity of the injury does not exceed the following: post-traumatic amnesia for greater than 24 hours, after the first 20 minutes the Glasgow Coma Score is 13 – 15, and a loss of consciousness is less than 20 minutes."

An individual can sustain a concussion with or without a blow to the head. Your brain sits inside your skull surrounded by cerebral spinal fluid and meninges that naturally absorb minor shocks to the head. When a concussion occurs, the brain slams into the bony protuberances inside of the skull. These accelerations cause the gray and white matter to move at different rates, creating axonal strain and damage to the neurolemma. Once a concussion occurs, the impact causes what is called a neurometabolic chain of events, involving a cascade of chemical reactions. These changes trigger a slowing of cerebral blood flow and ultimately cause energy depletion. This entire recovery process could take days to weeks to longer as the brain remains in a state of metabolic depression.

I like to remind parents that a concussion is like a snowflake. No two are alike in terms of the initial presentation, symptom severity, or recovery period. The aspects of concussion are similar, however, and are most often grouped into vestibular, ocular motor, neurocognitive and psychological symptoms. The cognitive symptoms of concussion include difficulty thinking clearly, feeling slowed down, difficulty with concentration and reduced memory. Physical symptoms of concussion include a headache, nausea, vomiting, balance problems, dizziness, blurred vision, fatigue, sensitivity to light and sensitivity to noise. Emotional symptoms include irritability, emotional lability, sadness, and nervousness. Sleep disturbances such as difficulty falling asleep, sleeping more than usual and sleeping less than usual are common as well.

True statements:

"When I was a kid, and you got knocked out, they just woke you up, and you kept right on playing."

"I have been heading the soccer ball my whole life, and look at me, I am fine. My daughter will be too."

"Yes, I know my son has a concussion, but he only has a headache, and he has a tournament next week."

"The doctor told me to rest a day, and I would be fine by Monday. The CT scan was negative."

These statements are made by loving, well-meaning, dedicated parents that have not yet been well informed or have been misinformed regarding the process and recovery from concussion. In my practice, we feel we have achieved success when we have dispelled these myths and replaced them with good, solid, scientifically driven data and information. Without understanding concussion, our parents and our community may inadvertently make our children vulnerable to the lifelong effects associated with repeated concussion. Sadly, I have seen too many cases of kids who have had to leave their favorite sports because they have previously had multiple concussions that were mismanaged or unrecognized.

And even more unsettling are the subsequent cognitive difficulties and learning challenges that accompany multiple concussions.

As youth sports have changed, our children are considered more at risk for concussion than ever before. A generation ago, children played on recreational teams that met one to two times per week. Now, our children are playing on club teams and school teams, as well as participating in hours of private training and practice. Also, girls are playing more contact sports such as lacrosse and ice hockey, than ever before. The increase in games and practice and athletic exposures puts children at greater risk for physical and head injuries. In addition, there is greater player variability regarding size, strength, and ability at younger ages that put them at further risk for injury.

It was once thought that the younger the child, the more resistant they would be to the effects of a brain injury. That they could "bounce back" quicker than adults. Now we know that this could not be further from the truth, as children are without a doubt more vulnerable to concussion than adults. This has been further evidenced in animal models that show the developing brain is more vulnerable and displays a slower recovery pattern than the adult fully developed brain (Giza and Hovda, 2001.)

What makes a child more vulnerable? It is theorized that anatomical and physiological factors such as smaller head mass, rapid brain development, and age-related differences in brain recovery mechanisms largely account for their higher risk. Also, the younger the child is, the more challenging the assessment and evaluation of concussion is. There is not only a paucity of objective cognitive tests for children, but it is also difficult to assess subjective symptoms due to their level of intellect and understanding at the time of the injury. How many eight-year-olds do you know that can adequately describe their experience of memory loss or mental fogginess?

Older children and adolescents are also infamous for purposely underreporting concussion symptoms, making the objective assessment of concussion invaluable. In an often cited study by Michael McCrea in 2004, high school students were surveyed about why they did not report concussion symptoms to their high school coaches or parents. The study found that 66 percent of the athletes did not feel their injury was serious enough, 41 percent did not want to leave the game, 36 percent did not know they had a concussion, and 22 percent did not want to let their team down. As concussion laws have been implemented across high schools nationwide, it is our hope that this "zone of silence," or fear of being viewed as weak by coaches and teammates will be eliminated.

The field of concussion is rapidly changing in terms of advances in science and research. Radiological advances continue to change our understanding of the effects of concussive and subconcussive blows that are not readily seen on a functional basis. That is, we now know that even when concussive symptoms are not reported, repeated blows to the head can cause structural changes in the brain that are not readily detected by our current methods of radiological assessment such as CT scan or MRI. And we have always known that neurons, our brain cells, do not regenerate once they are damaged.

As neuropsychologists in the field of brain injury and concussion management, we have a moral and ethical obligation to gain knowledge on the latest advances in the field of neuroscience and to share this information in such a way that is useful and meaningful to those who need it the most.

"The meaning of life is to find your gift. The purpose in life is to give it away."

William Shakespeare

About Kristine C. Keane, Psy.D.

Dr. Kristine Keane is a Clinical Neuropsychologist who is the director of a multi-specialty private practice that serves adults, adolescents and children with a variety of neuropsychological and psychological disorders. The practice has three locations serving Monmouth and Ocean County and employs Neuropsychologists, Clinical Psychologists, Counselors, Speech Pathology Therapists and Biofeedback therapists. Dr. Keane is a consulting Neuropsychologist at Jersey Shore University Medical Center, Ocean Medical Center, Shore Rehabilitation Institute, and Laurel Rehabilitation. She is also the Clinical Director of the Meridian Concussion Program and provides concussion education to physicians, psychologists, medical staff, educators, coaches and athletes. She volunteers for the Brain Injury Association of New Jersey and is on the Board of the Youth Sports Concussion Committee which involves creation of legislation, concussion education and community awareness. She has been actively treating and assisting Traumatic Brain Injury patients and their families for the past fifteen years.

Contact Kristine Today!

Shore Neuropsychology and Behavioral Health
220 Jack Martin Boulevard Unit E2
Brick, New Jersey 08724

Email: kkeane@shoreneuropsych.com

Phone: 732-920-3434

Fax: 732-920-2447

Chapter 14

Breakup to Breakthrough

Authored by Rosanne S. DeTorres, Esq.

My parents were the children of Italian immigrants. From my dad's perspective, he thought of my work as two people battling it out in court with one person winning and one person losing. He would often ask me, "Did you win in court today?" And I would tell him, "Dad, no one wins in divorce. Everybody loses."

I tell my clients that the best result in any divorce is a settlement that honors the integrity of both spouses and elevates the interests of the children, if any. The best settlement is therefore the one where each spouse leaves the process equally unhappy. No one should be thrilled and no one should be completely devastated.

I also tell my clients that they have to weigh their desire to achieve a particular outcome against the time, energy, and money to achieve that result. Only they can decide how much to exert. A divorce attorney's job is to help clients weigh alternatives and provide insights for them to make informed decisions.

My practice is dedicated exclusively to family law. I help men and women navigate the intensely emotional process of divorce. I have been doing this for twenty-seven years. Everyone has a unique story to tell with nuanced dynamics, facts, and timelines. As a trusted and specialized divorce attorney, I listen carefully to clients' stories and provide sound legal advice. My objective is to guide them toward the best course of action and outcome - for them and their loved ones.

In the twenty-seven years I have served clients, I have consistently seen three areas worth thinking through for anyone considering divorce. If I were going through this significant life-altering event, I would feel grateful towards an attorney that clued me in on the following: 1. Prepare yourself, 2. Select the right lawyer, and 3. Be flexible.

One: Prepare Yourself

The door to your divorce attorney's office is potentially the heaviest one you may ever open. To even consider entering, you have likely grieved the loss of your relationship and made the decision to dissolve the marriage. Perhaps you have done enough "letting go" to consider divorce and want to learn more about what to expect. In either scenario, the best advice I can give is to mindfully prepare for the divorce process. Prepare emotionally, financially, and socially.

Emotionally

The process of divorce is intensely emotional for most people. The emotional ups and downs get worse before they get better, particularly if you continue to live with your spouse during the process. There is no shame in seeking professional help to honor, express, and manage your feelings. An experienced therapist can help tremendously with insights and skills to effectively communicate with your spouse. Managing your emotional needs is not a divorce lawyer's role.

Financially

If you are not the breadwinner in your marriage or have little understanding of the economic realities of your marriage, spend some time learning about your financial situation prior to contacting a lawyer. Start collecting information and documents, even if you have to do it quietly without your spouse knowing. Begin to put a folder together that includes: tax returns, W-2's, 1099's, pay stubs, corporate benefit statements, insurance policies, statements for bank accounts, stock accounts and retirement accounts, statements for all debts including mortgages, lines of credit, auto loans or leases and credit cards. Scan the mail as it comes in and make copies. If you are not sure if a document, statement, or bill is relevant, copy it anyway. Your attorney will be glad you did because it helps when evaluating your case and your rights properly and efficiently.

Socially

Prepare a support team. For many divorcing people, the loss of the marriage also means a loss of friends and a diminishing of your support network. Do your best to build a support network of friends and social resources. It is good to have this network in place when you need to talk to someone besides a therapist. This network can include family members, friends, or a spiritual advisor. I also suggest that this network include some stress relieving mechanisms such as physical exercise. My personal favorite is swimming, cycling, and running - any form of physical exercise will raise your endorphin levels and ease the psychological stress.

Two: Select The Right Lawyer

When you hire an experienced divorce attorney, you are paying for their proven skills, subject matter expertise, and their creative ability to solve your particular issues.

I have worked with people after they did their own divorce to fix things they did not understand or consider carefully enough. Non-attorneys simply do not have the skills and subject matter expertise to foresee the myriad of consequences and possibilities that can occur in the divorce process. If you have anything of significance at stake, if you have children, are a dependent spouse, own a business, are a significant wage earner, or have any assets of value, please do not consider representing yourself in the divorce. The risks and stakes are simply too high to leave your family's and your future to chance.

If you have anything of significance at stake in your divorce, do not hire a general practitioner to handle your case. Look for a certified specialist that keeps up with complex and continually changing divorce laws. If you hire a generalist, the nuances of how laws apply to your case will likely go unseen.

To be certain you are hiring an experienced divorce attorney, select a board certified specialist in divorce or matrimonial law. Many states have specialty certification programs administered by their bar association or law licensing board. These state programs also require specialists to be re-certified every few years to stay on top of the latest developments in the law. In New Jersey where I practice, I am certified by the New Jersey Supreme Court as a Matrimonial Law attorney. To achieve this designation, colleagues and judges evaluated me. I also had to pass a rigorous exam and prove involvement in numerous settled and litigated cases. I also have to be re-certified every few years.

Once you identify several certified matrimonial law attorneys, interview them carefully. Pay attention to all of your interactions with the lawyer and staff. Consider bringing a friend or family member with you to the initial meetings, even if you are not feeling nervous. A second set of eyes and ears can be very helpful. After the meeting, reflect on how client-centric the experience was. The following questions can be used as a guide to evaluate how dedicated, determined, and dependable your potential lawyer will be.

- Did the person on the initial phone call answer your questions patiently and schedule an initial meeting with flexibility?

- Were you greeted upon arrival and made to feel welcome?

- Was the environment organized and clean?

- How was the rapport with the attorney you met?

- Did s/he invite you to ask questions and answer all of yours?

- Did s/he appear to understand the issues unique to your case?

- Did s/he provide an outline of their process and approach?

Three: Be Flexible

A specialized divorce attorney will evaluate your case facts. S/he will tell you what you are entitled to and likely to achieve should a judge need to decide your case. A seasoned attorney will also negotiate the best possible solutions to the issues in your case and provide you with creative solutions to resolve impasses and breakdowns in the settlement process. 98-99% of all divorce couples settle their divorce through negotiation and compromise without the involvement of a court or judge. This means that your divorce attorney's primary role is as an advisor and counselor to guide you to the outcome that is best for your family and you. All this being said, no divorce attorney can get you to the final settlement without a client who is willing to be flexible.

A seasoned divorce lawyer…has the depth of experience to understand all the different ways your case can be settled and guide you through that process, will tell you what your spouse's position is likely to be on any particular issue and how your spouse is likely to respond to your settlement position, and will be able to craft fallback positions to those objections and help you develop a "Plan B" to resolve issues in dispute.

"No matter how hard the past, you can always begin again. "

Buddha.

About Rosanne S. DeTorres, Esq.

I practice matrimonial law to help people make critical life transitions with the least stress possible. This takes strong ears and the creative capacity to help my client's reach their financial, support, custody and parenting goals. I didn't start out as a matrimonial lawyer. As a single parent in Maryland in the mid-eighties, I used my law degree to manage legal and business transactions for a large real estate firm. While this was rewarding, I decided to move back home to New Jersey where I had the support of my family and where I taught myself the nuances of divorce and family law.

Today, I'm the managing partner of DeTorres & DeGeorge – a niche family law firm in Flemington, New Jersey where 100 clients are annually given top-shelf guidance to transition and transform their lives into their own creations. My background in business transactions and ownership also comes in handy. It uniquely qualifies D and D to reach smart, amicable matrimonial solutions that involve family businesses.

- New Jersey Supreme Court Matrimonial Law Attorney

- 2015 Top 100 Family Lawyer in the State of New Jersey

- 2015 & 2016 New Jersey Super Lawyers List

- Member, Executive Committee of the Family Law Section, NJ State Bar Association

- Trustee, Business Women Networking, Inc.

- Member, Women President's Organization

Contact Rosanne Today!

Website: http://danddfamilylaw.com

Email: Rosanne@danddfamilylaw.com

Phone: 908-284-6005

Chapter 15

The Feng Shui Breakthrough

Authored by Lois Kramer-Perez CHt.

Any time before 2000, if you had told me by 2007, I would be a Feng Shui Practitioner leading Guided Clearing Meditation Classes among other things, I would have looked at you like you were crazy. Before Sept 2000, I was an obsessed woman in the fashion business, consumed with the pursuit of perfect sweaters, traveling around the world. I loved this industry as it gave me an opportunity to work with some of the most creative designers in the field. I needed to be in a creative environment to keep my juices flowing, and this was the perfect fit!

I was so revved up all the time, I just couldn't shut it down, even going to the movies was a challenge. With ants in my pants I always sat on the aisle so I could get up and walk around! Although fulfilled, I would say to my husband, Ray, "When I turn 50, I want to leave this wacky world and do *something* just because I love it, without the stress, without the pressure." I had no idea what *that something* would be, because I loved what I was doing; but I recognized that change would be coming soon. Ah, I had no idea what was coming.

In Sept 2000, my husband of 19 years suffered a heart attack at home and never recovered. My life would change forever, and I was just 46.

At first I allowed the pursuit of the perfect sweater to consume me, but then I started to look for something more. I was craving something to ease the pain, something to help me get back to living. I began to notice things in a different way. I felt as if I was being directed to look in another direction. My eyes began to open up to see what was showing up in front of me. I stumbled into a Reiki Studio; the teacher was awaiting, and my transformation began. I absorbed Reiki like a sponge. I found an inner peace I never knew existed. As I healed within, continuing my studies, I became a Reiki Master Practitioner, not ever expecting I would heal anyone other than myself.

My curiosity was piqued when I attended a class *Clear Your Clutter with Feng Shui*. Sounds good to me. If Reiki can help you find peace and balance from within, why not create an environment to find balance to support what is going on from the outside. I began my Feng Shui Certification program in 2003. I was to learn *As Within, So Without*. What is going on *inside of us* is being reflected *outside of us* in our space.

When I completed my first year of Feng Shui Certification in 2004, I was 50! I also found a nod of approval from my late husband, Ray, as I began my journey. Preparing for a class where I was learning about the *I Ching*, I found a book in Ray's office, *The Illustrated I Ching*. Wow! I had no idea what this was, let alone that I would find the book I needed right there in my home.

My life was truly changing. I learned how we are always creating "imprints," the patterns in our life. When we become consciously aware of our unconscious actions, we begin to notice the feelings that become "imprinted" in our automatic response system. As we purposefully create the experiences we choose to imprint, we are setting our automatic response system to create those feelings, to attract the choices we welcome into our life.

I felt liberated! I realized the things about me that made me unique were wonderful, not something to be ashamed of. I relished the fact that *I was not a bedroom-set kinda' girl!* Growing up I believed that once you got married, you bought a bedroom set, set up your household and became an adult. Well, I was married for 19 years and never found a bedroom set that I loved.

Feng Shui taught me I did not have to hold on to a belief that no longer served me. I bought a fabulous bed with a headboard and footboard, one year later I found the perfect end tables, and one year after that, a dresser that I still adore.

Whenever I get stuck and find myself not able to move forward, I smile and say – *I am not a bedroom set kinda' girl.* It is okay to do it my way as long as I am doing!

Looking back on my life, I know it was no accident I was cast as Peter Pan in my 5th-grade school play! I was and still am comfortable in my own skin, and may never grow up to be the adult I thought I had to be. I am enjoying just being me!

With this new freedom, I began to live my life very differently. Buying that new bed was powerful as well as some of the other changes I made in my home. The more I studied, the more excited I was to share my knowledge. I began teaching at night and Feng Shui consulting on the weekends. Still working in pursuit of the perfect sweater, my approach changed from obsession to passion with an element of Feng Shui-fun! I began daydreaming how great I felt as a full-time Feng Shui practitioner. Could I leave my pursuit of the perfect sweater? My elaborate daydreams consisted of not only envisioning my new life, but with each class that I taught, and with each Feng Shui consultation I completed, I experienced living this energy fully. The reality was getting closer.

My answer would come clearly on a business trip to Asia in December, 2006. Traveling with the design team, we arrived in Shanghai from Seoul, Checking into the hotel, I couldn't get my hands on my passport. Hmm, I'll go to my room and empty my bag. Nope, not there. Back down to the lobby, I explained to the concierge that I must have dropped my passport in the customs area at the airport. Could he please check to see if it was found? I gave the concierge my information, told him I was going out to dinner, and I would return at 11:00 pm. I was confident when I returned he would say "Good news, Mrs. Kramer-Perez! Good things happen to people. We found your passport!" He looked at me as if I had lost my mind, but politely smiled and said, "Of course."

It took all my strength using all I had learned these past few years, NOT to give into the panic that began to rise in my throat. I kept visualizing myself walking into the lobby, hearing the concierge speak those words with a smile on his face. I *felt* it happen. There was no other outcome I would accept. My traveling companions were kind but somewhat skeptical. When I did return that evening at 11:00 pm, the concierge had a huge smile on his face as I approached the front desk. He proclaimed, "Good news Mrs. Kramer-Perez. Good things happen to people. We found your passport!"

I knew then what I had to do. I was so excited to return after the holiday break to resign. Things began to delay my resignation. First, I had to wait for my direct report to return from traveling, and then I was told I would be let go as they were restructuring, and I should wait until I was offered a package. I waited two more weeks, and then I decided, I am going on my terms, in my way. I felt empowered handing in my resignation, knowing that one chapter was closing, and another chapter was beginning. My last day in the office was Chinese New Year's Eve! Divine. The timing was perfect. Filled with passion, there was no room for fear.

In February 2007, as I left my pursuit of the perfect sweater, I began my new life becoming the driver of my destiny.

So what's the point of all of this? What's Feng Shui got to do with it? Everything! The principles of Feng Shui opened my eyes in more ways than I ever could have imagined. It is a magical gift of noticing all of the opportunities continuously showing up before me. And I am the one responsible for my choices.

What is the link to all of these stories? Participation. Do something.

We can dream it, but we must believe it with all of our heart, with every breath and fill up every cell in our bodies. Filled with our knowing, we cannot help but participate with action. Allowing it to draw us in, we move forward. We must do something to keep those fires burning.

Einstein told us *"nothing happens unless something moves."*

Doing something is better than doing nothing. Whenever I get stuck and find myself doing nothing, I smile as I know very well, *"I am not a bedroom set kinda' girl!"* and the possibilities are endless.

Are you ready to participate with me? Unleash your possibilities, experience the transformation within. Begin your breakthrough now at loiskrameperez.com, get results.

About Lois Kramer-Perez CHt.

Lois Kramer-Perez CHt. is the go-to expert when you're finally ready to receive passionate relationships, a peaceful home, and a life you love. She puts her ten plus years of feng shui energy clearing to work for relators, divorcees, business owners, and busy women, to put them in the driver's seat with their relationships and spaces. She is a sought after speaker, expert, and author, and creator of popular programs such as "Clearing Meditation Circle" and the "Feng Shui Jumpstart." Lois is a faculty member at Emerson and Ridgewood Community Schools in NJ, a top contributor to *Inner Realm* and *Natural Awakenings* magazines, Pazoo.com's Feng Shui expert, PoweHerNetwork.com teacher and sits on the board of the International Feng Shui Guild. Lois is a graduate of Fashion Institute of Technology, Feng Shui Alliance School and Institute of Hypnotherapy.

Contact Lois Today!

Feng Shui Your Space and Your Soul.

Website: http://loiskramerperez.com

Email: lois@loiskramerperez.com

Phone: 201-906-5767

Chapter 16

Seven Website MUST-HAVES for Breakthrough Results

Authored by Jayne Rios

In today's world, you need a website that is professional. You have seven seconds to make a first impression online. 85% of people buy from first-page search engine results, and the Internet is the number one tool prospects use to find you! Having a monetized website is crucial to your success.

Do you have to spend thousands of dollars to create it? Not really. I am going to show you the must-haves for your site so that you do not "buy" more than is needed. If you already have a website, these tips will help you learn how to 1) optimize your site to build an opt-in list 2) create landing pages to increase your Search Engine Optimization and much more. We also teach this in our www.entrepreneur360.com training as well. Here's to your success online!

Seven Website MUST-HAVES When Using the Internet to Get Breakthrough Results:

1. Website URL (Universal Resource Locator) **is Key**

Most people around the world use a browser bar to search for what they want on the internet. Therefore, a good website name will include your top keywords. These keywords should match what people are using to search for your product or service.

Here's how to choose a website URL:

- Use Google's Keyword Planner Tool to search for your top keywords (these are the words your customers use to find you).

- Make a list of your top choices based on the most searched keywords relative to your product or service.

- Go to www.godaddy.com, enter your selections and search to see if any URL's are available.

- Once you have found your best website URL option, buy it. (I would also suggest buying your name. One of my URL's is www.jaynerios.com).

2. Opt-in Email Form

Now that you have your Website name/URL, it's time to get down to business. The number one item you will need on your website is an email opt-in form. This is how you are going to build an opt-in list and create your email list for marketing.

Capture Contact Information

When visitors come to your site but don't call or buy anything, it is important for you to at least try to capture their contact information. The way you do that is by offering a gift. When they sign up, you now have their name and email so that you can send follow-up emails or autoresponders. (Emails that are automatically sent nurture the customer until they are ready to buy.)

Make an Offer They Can't Refuse

The most effective way to solicit contact information is to offer something that is not only free but valuable to your audience. The more necessary and valuable the information, the better your chances of growing your opt-in list, and converting visitors to buyers or clients

3. **Contact Us information**

Your contact information should include a company phone number, email, and contact form to complete for additional information. Unfortunately, I have seen too many companies provide only a contact form on their website. Basically, here's what they are saying: "Dear Visitor: We are too important and too busy to talk to you at your convenience. Please take your time to fill out this form and submit to us. We'll decide when it's convenient for us to respond to you." Did they ever stop and think they are not the only one in the world providing that product or service? By providing a phone number on your website, you will have the advantage of being there during the customer's 30-minute window of BUY TIME. Without a phone number, you may miss out on a sales opportunity.

If you have a home-based business, sign-up for an 800 number that only charges when you use it (initially, this may be only $5.00 per month). As your business grows, you'll find it worthwhile to pay the $9.95 per month for unlimited calls. If you have a business phone, be sure to add it to your website!

4. Video

Create a video overview about your company and services. Statistics show that 85% of web viewers prefer to watch a quick overview video than read content. After watching the video, interested viewers will want more information, and they will read your content. But you can capture them right off the bat with a video. Video is also a powerful tool for Search Engine Optimization (SEO).

Video Production

In today's marketplace, a business video does not need to have high production value. YouTube changed the game for all marketers. You can now use a SmartPhone or handheld camera to produce an effective video. You can also create an inexpensive video by visiting Animoto, Camtasia, and many others.

The types of videos you can create on your Smartphone are endless:

- Company Overview
- Customer Testimonies

- Product Demonstrations

- White Papers

- Case Studies

- Webinar Recordings

- Opt-in Campaign

- Short Vlogs

To learn more about, and find step-by-step instructions to help you create dynamic marketing programs from your Smartphone, upload video into YouTube, produce landing pages and more, check out my eCourses on http://expressyourselfelearning.com.

5. Customer Testimonies

Customer testimonies are powerful sales tools on a website, and they can help establish your credibility. They can either be video testimonies or typed quotes. People want to hear from others, and to be assured you can do what you say you can do. A great customer testimony tells how you provided a solution to a client's problem, or how you met a specific need. No one wants to hear how great you are. They want to hear what you can do for them!

6. One Click Away

This is the golden rule. Everything you are offering should be one click away from the homepage. What does this mean? When visitors come to your site, they usually land on your homepage. If you are selling products or services, they should be highlighted here. When the visitor clicks the link to find out more, they should find on the new page:

- Exactly what was promised
- A way to contact you by phone, email, contact form or social media.
- A Buy Now button (if you are offering a product for sale)

7. Social Media buttons

Many people will feel more comfortable connecting with you through social media than picking up the phone and calling, or completing a contact form. So, make it easy for visitors to contact you by displaying your social media icons with links on every page. Social media offers a unique opportunity to establish a relationship with your visitor before he or she buys.

If you have these seven key elements in place on your website, you are ready to begin your Breakthrough Journey! If not, keep reading to learn how to put the pieces in place.

Website Newbies (Things to remember)

Search Engine Optimization

Flash sites like wix.com and the free sites through vistaprint.com won't help you get found on the search engines. Creating your website in Wordpress is the easiest, most cost-effective way for you to get a website up in under one week (as long as you have a logo and content). In addition to the cost and ease-of-use benefits, search engines love Wordpress! Go to wordpress.com to learn more!

Cost

You don't have to spend a fortune on a website. There are website developers who can build a nice website for under $1,500. Do your research, ask for references, and negotiate. Take the list above with you to the meeting to ensure these items are included in the estimate. We can also help you, check our sites out at www.expressyourselfelearning.com. In our 12 month VIP program, we actually do the work for you.

Review the below Website Checklist and make sure you have all the pieces in place. If you do not have one of these, challenge yourself. Find out how you can create it and make it happen!

Website Checklist:

- SEO Friendly URL

- Contact Information Updated

- Promotions on Home Page

- Opt-in Form on pages where it makes sense

- Social Media buttons

- Customer Testimonies

- Video

- Everything is One Click Away

- About Us Section (great to have Mission Statement, Vision and Management Links)

- Products page with Buy Now Buttons (if applicable)

- Good Content with Calls to Action

Summary

Of course, there are many more tricks we use to have a high converting website; however, in this short chapter, I wanted to give you the MUST-HAVES! And, as you know, the website is only one piece of achieving the gold and getting you even better Breakthrough Results. In our programs, we help you structure your business for success, including money management, millionaire mindset, automated systems, passive income opportunities and much more. Please visit our website at:

www.entrepreneur360success.com to learn more.

About Jayne Rios

Jayne Rios is the Internationally known bestselling author of *Interactive Author: Monetize Your Message*, CEO of Express Yourself eLearning and Co-founder of Women's Global Leadership Alliance (womensgla.com). She hosts an internet TV show and speaks nationally.

Jayne's passion is to empower and equip entrepreneurs and small business owners by providing the tools and resources needed to turn a passion into a movement and/or online business. By using her successful background in the areas of internet marketing, video, and eLearning, she helps implement online solutions that work.

To learn more about Jayne visit her website at www.entrepreneur360success.com or to collaborate with global women visit www.womensgla.com. You can always email Jayne for a quicker response at jayne@womensgla.com.

Contact Jayne Today!

Website: http://www.entrepreneur360success.com

Email: jayne@womensgla.com

Chapter 17

How Should You Start Using Social Media for Your Business? Forget About Social Media, Seriously!

Authored by David Deutsch

There are many misconceptions when it comes to social media. One of the most common is some variation of the following:

- "I want a Facebook page and 10,000 Likes!"

- "I need a LinkedIn account with 500+ connections!"

- "I want to be on Twitter and get more 'Likes' 'Followers' and 'Shares'!"

After hearing this over and over from prospective clients for over five years, I realized something.

These people were lying to me.

Okay, maybe lying is a bit harsh.

In reality, they weren't lying, so much as not completing their sentences. The rest of their sentences were, or at least should have been: "I want a Facebook page, a LinkedIn account and I want to Tweet *so my company can, somehow, make more money.*"

Let Theodore Levitt illustrate:

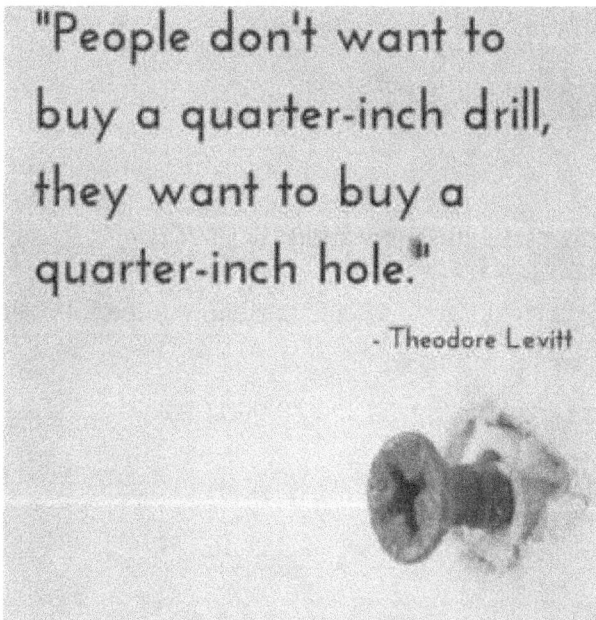

"People don't want to buy a quarter-inch drill, they want to buy a quarter-inch hole."

- Theodore Levitt

So no, you do not want a Facebook page, a LinkedIn account or a Twitter feed with lots of likes, followers, and shares. That's just a quarter-inch drill. You really want to earn more money. That's your quarter-inch hole.

How can you do this? Forget about social media for a moment. Seriously. Pretend it doesn't exist.

Now that you have mentally destroyed LinkedIn list your business objectives and *apply social media tools to those objectives.* Examples of business objectives include, but are not limited to:

1. More leads

2. Better quality leads

3. Improve partner work performance

4. Increased employee productivity / decreased employee turnover

It is not easy to implement these objectives. After all, odds are you didn't start your business so you can Tweet. Indeed, if it were easy, everyone would be doing it.

Know Your Goals

Recently a colleague said to me, "I want to create buzz about my product."

So I asked her, "What does 'create buzz' mean to you?"

"Well," she said, "I want people to talk about my product."

"And," I continued, "If people talk about your product, then what?"

She quickly knew where I was going: simply having others talk about your business is great.

But, can buzz pay your bills?

Folks, buzz is for bees. You want the honey. And the honey is money.

However, when you start with business *goals*, you end up with business *results*. And, hopefully, complete sentences.

Defining Social Media

To make things easy for you, I have defined social media in just two words:

Interactivity

Narcissism

Let's break these down, shall we?

Interactivity: There are two levels of interactivity when it comes to social media: speaking and listening. Many firms mistakenly believe they should go on social media to promote themselves. Ladies and gentlemen, *this is exactly the wrong way to use social media*. Using social media effectively means listening more than speaking and engaging in conversations with your audience, not promoting your stuff to them.

Narcissism: Although this is said somewhat in jest, there is an important point to be made which I make over and over: get to know your audience and give them what they want. For instance, I am not a sports fan at all. Sports bore me to tears. Frankly, I'd rather do just about anything than watch a game. So if you start describing details about college football statistics, I'm gone in like two seconds. However, I am a social media junky. If I start talking to you, dear reader, about social media and you don't care one whit about it, I will lose you.

To draw an analogy, think of your website as your workplace and social media as the bar after work.

Social Media is Not Marketing. It is a Conversation. In fact, social media is nothing more than people talking to people using technology.

Think of it this way: if you are at your local bar, would you like it if someone from a car company jumped in the middle of your conversation and started selling you a car? You'd be annoyed, right?

Of course, you would be, and you should be. There is no difference here on social media.

So, the lesson for you today: One-half of the term social media is social. So, use it to talk to people and, more importantly, listen to them! Many professionals dislike self-promotion anyway, so instead start talking to people about your passion or helping businesses, etc.

And, don't ask me what the future of social media is. If I could read the future, I would be a multi-billionaire.

The Power of Social Media Listening

Believe it or not, you can generate a lot of value from social media by saying nothing, but instead listening to what others are saying about you, your industry and your competitors.

In fact, some firms have set up social media war rooms whose full-time job is to monitor and respond to social media comments. In other words, they have embraced the concept that social media is much more than speaking: they see the hard-dollar value of listening and responding as well.

Here are a few examples of how this works:

- A couple of years ago I went to visit a client on-site to work on their nascent social media strategy. When I arrived, my client had a very frustrated look and tone about her. When I asked what was wrong, she said, "I am having trouble getting (Large Telecommunications Company Which Begins With V and Rhymes with Horizon but Shall Not be Named) to respond to my problem. The service isn't working, and they overbilled me." She was more than frustrated and could not focus on our session.

"Send them a tweet," I casually suggested. As soon as I finished my sentence she looked at me like I had three heads. "Seriously, this could be a great lesson how to use social media effectively."

Finally, she agreed to send them a tweet. Within minutes, she received a response from them. A week later she said she received the best customer service of her life, and her issue was resolved quickly and professionally.

- A colleague of mine told me about an issue he had with his tractor that was not resolved. He took to LinkedIn, found the person in charge of customer complaints and reached out directly to him.

The director took my colleague's contact information and, within four minutes, was put in touch with the customer service team who immediately got on the ball. And he had the best experience of his life.

- Your humble author recently had a problem with LinkedIn, my go-to network for lead generation. Apparently they removed an important feature that upset me greatly.

The first thing I did was post questions on my personal Facebook page, as well as a Facebook group specifically for social media professionals. Nobody could figure out what to do next. So instead of sending LinkedIn a private request I took to Twitter and had the following exchange with them

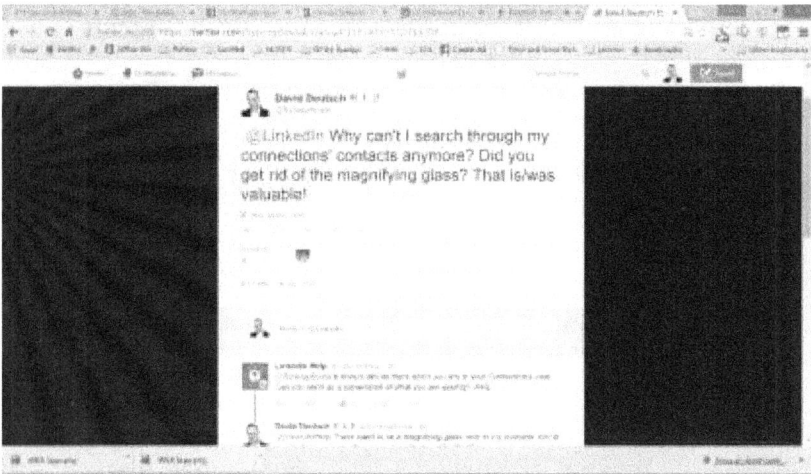

And here is the response I received, along with the rest of our conversation:

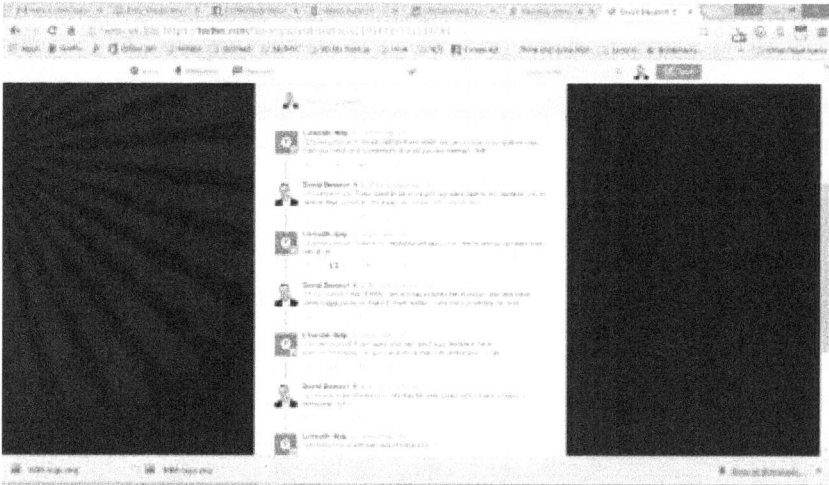

How are these companies able to monitor such conversations? Believe it or not, there are social media listening tools that crawl social media for the conversations they are interested in. One of the most popular social listening tools is Radian[6]. If you cannot afford to invest in tools like R^6 you can start with free tools such as Topsy or SocialMention to start listening to conversations and upgrade later.

This is not the world of the future folks. All kinds of conversations about your industry, and possibly your firm, are happening all the time on social media. And if you are not listening to what people are saying, you might be missing out on potentially huge opportunities to grow your business, respond to customer concerns and offer something you never even considered before.

What You Can Do Right Now

You have many opportunities to generate business with social media. The technical details of how to use it misses the point. Instead, focus your time and energy on finding the right message. And that message should be about listening and engaging, not self-promoting: give to your audience instead of getting stuff from them, and build a good reputation off-line to enhance your experience online.

My suggestion is to simply get on there and share content with your networks which has nothing to do with you, such as:

- Job openings at other firms
- Thanking your colleague(s) for good work they did
- Writing recommendations on LinkedIn
- Sharing useful articles for your current and prospective clients
- Ask and answer questions

You'll probably find this approach far less stressful and, in the long-run, more profitable. So don't let fear stop you, take charge and do it!

About David Deutsch

In a nutshell, David is a serial failure. Some of his flubs, missteps, and mess-ups include: having never held a full-time job for longer than 1½ years; nearly flunking out of Community College; (mis) managing two rock-and-roll bands that went absolutely nowhere; dropping out of culinary school; and that's just for starters! Every so often, he accidentally does not fail. Such successes-in-spite-of-himself include: spending an academic year in China, learning Mandarin Chinese; starting a business called SynergiSocial; aligning his firm with Whitman Business Advisors; writing this book section, and meeting amazing people like his co-authors. He lives in Flemington, NJ.

Contact David Today!

Website: http://www.synergisocial.com

Email: david@synergisocial.com

Phone: 973-879-9654

Twitter: @SynergiSocial

LinkedIn: http://www.linkedin.com/in/davidldeutsch

Chapter 18

Who's Who and What's What? The Representative has arrived!

Authored by MJ Cunningham

So who is who? Who is the Representative? At a very basic

level, a Representative is someone who is chosen to act or speak on the behalf of someone else. They may or may not fully believe in what they are representing or be fully committed to what they are representing, but they look the part, talk the part, act the part. Sound familiar? Well in relationships (personal and business), they are someone who creates an image that portrays the characteristics that appeal to you. Their goal is often to get you to "yes" at any cost. We often describe the Representative in terms of "putting our best foot forward" code for – let's look perfect, act perfect, be perfect and they are sure to be mine! Oh, my.

Well, you might be wondering why the Representative shows up? In my experience, the Representative shows up because of an embedded fear within ourselves of not being good enough. Not good enough for ourselves and so not good enough for someone we want to impress. So we often are the Representative, who is involved with the Representative of another person. Again, we call this putting our best foot forward, thinking we are creating the best situation for now, yet, we are often not realizing we are only setting ourselves and our partners up for future catastrophes. I believe it is always a catastrophe when we are not true to ourselves. Yes, a catastrophe! I know you are thinking, that is a little dramatic, a catastrophe. And yes, I hope that word jars you deep down to your core. According to *Collins Cobuild English Dictionary for Advanced Learners,* a catastrophe is "an unexpected event that causes great suffering or damage." When we buy into the belief we are not good enough (often unknowingly), to reveal who we honestly are to someone we want to develop *the most intimate relationship* with, we set ourselves up for great suffering and damage. Again, it is my belief that when we are not true to ourselves, it is a catastrophe. Reflect on how you react to catastrophes we see more and more. Tsunamis, Earthquakes, Floods. We mourn, we try to make sense of it all, we pray, and we reach out to support those impacted, however, when we cover up who we are, when we do not like who we are, when we feel like we have to be "more" than who we are to please (catch), someone, it is truly a catastrophe. When we do not believe in our worthiness then how can we build a solid relationship? What is that? Now is a great time to break through this trap and recognize how to identify the Representative in ourselves.

Typically, you know in your heart and spirit that if it looks too good, sounds just right and acts on point all the time, look a little deeper **into yourself**. What fantasy are **you** creating and hoping for and why? It is that "perfect" image, what is said, how it is said, how does one look. Why? You know how much time you take to get yourself together so that everything is just right, perfect. Well, honestly, how sustainable is that? Further, when did we start to believe we could control it all? My challenge to you is look **deeper into yourself**. What is it within yourself that you are thirsting for that causes you to accept the fantasy and often contribute to the fantasy? Take a moment and chew on that. That is time well worth spending. The key is that by peeling back your onion you release yourself and open yourself up for an honest and true (not perfect), opportunity for intimacy. Also understood as "Into – Me – See." I think we so want to be and accept the Representative because we think that will allow us to get to a more intimate relationship quicker. Funny, that we can believe that by being unauthentic (fake), we can obtain and sustain a most prized, personal and most intimate relationship. Really?? Hmmm. My challenge to you, break through that fantasy and seek your authenticity.

Given the level of deception that accompanies the Representative, please be aware The Representative is quite dangerous. When we move away from the **value** of who we are (imperfections and all), we can lose touch with who we are. When we lose who we are, how can we truly connect and become one with someone else? The danger of losing yourself of hiding yourself is massive. When we cling to the Representative and only want to see the Representative in ourselves and our partner, we make critical decisions on perceived information. There is a saying that **"Perception is reality. If you are perceived to be something, you might as well be it because that's the truth in people's minds."** – *Steve Young.* Then sustaining that perception (aka the Representative), creates internal discord and eventually havoc. Living a life as a Representative can really escalate into a mess! The danger of being a Representative is that we create a blurred vision for ourselves and our partners. Blurred vision is not fun. Think about it, with blurred vision, one lacks sharpness of vision, resulting in the inability to see fine detail. (1) You cannot focus on much of anything, your depth perception is often compromised, you may have headaches, pain, and are not able to function properly and if you can, not for long. It is a rough place to be, blurred vision. We miss the fine details of ourselves and our partners. We just see the big picture, and not clearly. We miss the significant points that make you who you are and surely we are shielded from those fine points that make our partner who they are. So the challenge, how to get to your best-corrected vision and release the Representative that you present by looking deeper into yourself first and then looking deeper into your partner to look beyond both Representatives.

So now what? Take a step back and go deeper into seeing who you are. **Yes, start with you**! Go back and look for **your true self**. Identify your issues, your insecurities, bring your fears, hurt, and pain to the surface. Go back to identify as much as you can so you can move forward and Break Through to your true self of today. One of the most powerful methods is facing the past so you can understand it, **forgive it** and begin the journey of how you are fighting it in the present. This is your breakthrough that can take you to your "Best Corrected Vision" of who you are and what you are really looking for.

Your Best Corrected Vision. What does that mean? In the world of ophthalmology, at a very basic level, it is the vision one achieves using the correct prescription. That prescription can be achieved by using glasses/contacts/or through surgery (particularly laser), assuming all other parts of the eye are physically working. So how does that now connect to YOU? Well, you first have to acknowledge that you are not accepting or understanding who you are or perhaps accept that somewhere you think you are not good enough. Once you can accept that you have some work to do (that you can't see as clearly as you would like), then you get to work (go to the Ophthalmologist to get help). You have to start somewhere. Choose a place, any place. Start! In the doctor's office, you might start with 20/70 vision if the technician has no idea what your vision error is (refractive error). So we pick a place to start. If you can see something, we work from there. You know the drill, is it clearer – one or two? The same holds true for your self-assessment. What is truer to you – fear or insecurity, hurt or resentment, self-awareness or denial? Only you can recognize where those hot spots are, and only you can start to work on them. Often this comes with help. Invest in yourself and your future and get help to rewind so you can be free to spring forward. Remember, your best-corrected vision may not be perfect vision. Your best-corrected vision is not a Representative of you, it is YOU! You that sees more clearly and can be able to forgive, live and love you. That is not always 20/20, but the place where you can see correctly and on balance. It is well worth the trip to find your best self (and look for that in your partner). So, now what are you going to do? Break Through to today's you!

About MJ Cunningham

Married since 2002 to Bob Cunningham and enjoying many lively and adventurous years, MJ Cunningham is experiencing marriage live, up close and personal! She is the product of a 36 year marriage of her parents, ended early by the death of her father. With an MBA and MA Cunningham has spent her career cultivating relationships in sales, education and healthcare.

MJ is neither a marriage counselor nor a psychologist or psychiatrist. She is woman who has seen how she may have short circuited her own process embarking into THE most intimate and emotional relationship in her life. .Her first book, "So you feel like you want to get married, are you preparing for a certificate or covenant", will be released in 2016 and wants to provide another viewpoint on how one might consider stepping into and embracing the role of spouse.

Contact MJ Today!

Email: hopeandsuccessventures@gmail.com

Facebook: http://www.facebook.com/mj3enterprises/

Chapter 19

The Power of Dress, Image and Perception in the Workplace

Authored by Pamela Etzin

My story started a long time ago. I grew up in Buffalo, NY in the 1950's; a time when people took real pride in their appearance. It was very important to look proper, and my parents were always well dressed. For my mother, this meant a dress or a skirt and a full face of make-up. I could always count on my father to be wearing one of two outfits, either a dark suit with a white shirt and tie or casual slacks paired with his usual white shirt and v-neck cashmere sweater. Wherever they went, my parents commanded the room by the energy of their appearance. As a child, I never understood why people were always looking at them. But looking back with the knowledge of fashion I have acquired throughout my career, I have come to the realization that there was and still is a strong correlation between style and confidence. The better a person looks, the better a person feels. First impressions are everlasting, and our image can speak volumes about who we are or who we want to appear to be.

Does it really matter how I dress?

Yes! In 2012, a study in the Journal of Experimental Social Psychology coined the phrase "embodied cognition." Researchers concluded that our thoughts and actions are influenced by more than just our brains, but our body as well. Believe it or not, our wardrobe actually does have the power to impact both our physical job performance and the mental effect that our subconscious has on being successful and respected. Consider sleeping through your alarm, throwing on the first outfit you see, and rushing to get to work on time. Then picture waking up on time, planning out your day while eating breakfast, taking the time to get dressed, and arriving early to work. Which scenario do you think will result in a good day and which in a bad day? Feeling disorganized, disheveled and powerless is usually a package deal. But on the flip side, feeling powerful can be a result of being composed and well put together. Image is everything.

What does "Dress For Success" really mean?

Are you a high powered executive?

Do you speak in a board room?

Are you the face of the business?

Are you a woman business owner?

Are you entering the workforce for the first time, changing jobs, or making a career change?

Is your look current for today?

Any of those questions apply to you?

Dressing for success means knowing what you are dressing for. It means understanding the message that you are trying to convey and wearing clothes that look the part. Are you trying to attract clients to your company? Is there a dress code? What is the specialized industry look?

Dressing for the position means understanding that your appearance is going to play a significant role in the push from where you are now to where you want to be. Being capable of dressing yourself with the most flattering colors, features, and styles has the ability to impress and help seal the deal. Remember, looks speak volumes! So when you are shopping at the mall or getting dressed in the morning, keep in mind the question . . . what statement do you want to make?

Resistance to change/what your friends won't tell you.

One of the biggest problems I encounter in my initial meeting with clients is their hesitance to evolve with the times. With every season comes new, popular styles and colors of clothing, and it is important to stay up to speed with the current trends. In many cases, the men or women I work with are reluctant to try on different designs, patterns, and brands. To them, I ask: Do you think that you need to change you look? Have your friends hinted that a style update is just what you need, but have been scared to hurt your feelings? Are you overwhelmed at the thought of walking into a store and trying to figure out where to go and what you need? Is it just easier wearing what you already have in your closet?

The truth is it's easy to stay where we are, but often that is not the best option. Change can be difficult. Our wardrobes should change with the seasons and as our bodies and lifestyles change.

Are you waiting to lose weight before you shop?

Getting dressed in the morning can be a struggle for people who are trying to lose weight, and don't want to spend money on clothing that soon will not fit. In my opinion, this translates to putting your self-confidence on hold and punishing yourself until you reach a certain goal. I encounter this scenario with many clients, but it is a mistake! Feeling negative about your appearance every time you get dressed is not a healthy way to motivate yourself to lose weight. Rather, I tell my clients to sit down with me and create a list of short-term goals. We then strategize what types of clothing to buy that will not waste money, but will still accommodate their intentions and flatter their current body.

Is your clothing closet a mess?

A very popular phrase from those who hire me is, "My closet is a mess, and I feel like I have nothing to wear." The truth is your closet probably *does* need to be critiqued and evaluated. There are sure to be garments that you forgot about because they are hidden by unwanted clothing. We tend to hang on to clothing because we (used to) like it, it cost a lot of money or it brings back memories. You might not even know if it still fits you properly. If you have not worn a piece for a while, then you probably never will. By having a professional organize your closet, you will be able to see everything clearly from clothing to accessories to shoes. It doesn't serve you to hold onto it; it is a waste of valuable space in your closet and the time has come to let it go. Donate it and let someone else make good use of it. Building a wardrobe is about beginning with the versatile key pieces and adding on from there with accessories and seasonal pieces. Getting dressed in the morning should be stress-free and easy. This means walking into your closet and knowing what fits and looks great on you and knowing how to accessorize the outfit easily. Having a wardrobe that works for you is essential.

What's the difference between Style and Fashion?

Yves Saint Laurent once said, "Fashions Fade – Style is Eternal." This one sentence embodies all of the facets that make up my career as a personal stylist. Every season there are fashion "must haves," but that is not really what style is about. Style is a language, a quiet, unspoken message, an energy. It is making a personal statement to the world through your appearance!

Why Hire a Personal Stylist? I can do it myself

Sometimes, potential clients ask why they should hire a personal stylist and not just research and shop for clothes themselves. My answer is always the same. Often, how we see ourselves is not how we truly are. Because appearance is so crucial for professional success, investing in a wardrobe consultant is a worthy investment. You are not hiring me to pick clothes off of a rack, you are hiring me to consider your features and match the best styles, colors, and designers to best suit your body. You are hiring me to help build a sense of confidence that makes people turn when you walk into a room, just like people did for my parents. You are hiring me to make you look like your best self. And once this is done, you can truly accomplish anything.

I have had the great opportunity to share my passion and expertise with clients for many years, and it is rewarding every time. The one qualification for my clients is that they must have a willingness to put aside old beliefs and consider new possibilities! This is when the transformation can truly happen. After one session, I have seen a remarkable change in body language and watched individuals stand a little taller and smile in the mirror when they are genuinely satisfied at who is looking back at them.

So what are you waiting for? Ask yourself, do you feel great when you get dressed in the morning? Do you like how you look? Does your wardrobe reflect who you want to be?

Now is the time to step out of your comfort zone and embrace change.

Call or email me to receive a 30-minute complimentary style consultation and together, we can help you find your style!

About Pamela Etzin

Pamela Etzin is a Personal Stylist/Wardrobe Consultant and owner of An Eye For Detail. Prior to starting her styling business, Pamela spent over 39 years working on 7th Avenue in NYC's Garment Center, as well as for major retailers including Lord & Taylor, Talbots, and White House Black Market.

Pamela's strengths include, but are not limited to, helping men and women find their style while maintaining a look of confidence and success. In the words of an executive recruiter, "She is an incredible visionary, a chiropractor for your wardrobe and closet. Her enthusiasm is infectious, and her knowledge of fashion dare not be challenged."

Contact Pamela Today!

Website: http://www.eyefordetailnj.com

Email: pam@eyefordetailnj.com

Phone: 201-575-2626

Facebook: http://facebook.com/AnEyeForDetailNJ

LinkedIn : http://www.linkedin.com/in/pamelaetzin

Pinterest : http://www.pinterest.com/eyefordetailnj/l

Chapter 20

Luminous Communication: The Organic Dialogue that Sparkles

Authored by Wanda Harris

Communication is the essence of relationships whether inter- or intrapersonal. Finding ways to effectively communicate can invigorate dialogue and eliminate misunderstandings in our private and business life. The words we choose to use can be the difference between throwing dirt to a fire or sprinkling oil. Words hold power in the world of communication. Choosing to be powerful in examining, exploring and welcoming a new way to use words by making them bright, shining, and luminous will bring rewards in all aspects of your life.

The Luminous Communication approach that I will share with you opens the doors to so many advantages if failed dialogue, miscommunication and misconceptions have plagued your daily conversations. If you are willing to do some work and you are inspired to learn a new way of communicating, I will share some tips that will transform your relationships, your business, and your life. The Luminous Communication approach highlights possible dilemmas or problematic words and finds another way to present your thoughts in a clear, upbeat, positive and persuasive way. I will introduce you to a few techniques that will help you to transform your future dialogues.

Throughout this conversation, I will ask you to do some exercises focused on taking a critical look at how you may be communicating and how you can empower yourself to reinvent conversations.

Welcome to your new world, a new way of being and new forms of conversations: Luminous Communication, an engaging, interactive, revamped, incorruptible conversation. A dialogue that will spark aliveness, freshness and naturally stir the imagination while arming you with vital insights that are meaningful to your daily conversations. It simultaneously brings balance, ease and a peace of mind.

First, let's take a look at what governs communication. I think about four questions, what was said, how it was said, how it was heard and how it was interpreted. On many occasions, we have all heard one or more of these phrases, "That's not what I meant to say." "You took it the wrong way." "You don't listen to me." "What?" "Maybe I misunderstood." "That's not what I said." **Exercise**: *Think of a phrase that you've used or heard in your conversations where the communicator or listener was misunderstood, and the flow of conversation didn't go too well.*

The first technique of the Luminous Communication approach is to identify what we call "The Disconnect Dialogue."

The Disconnect Dialogue is recognizing when communication has failed you. Being aware that you didn't do the greatest job of getting your point across or truly listening to someone else. Were you stuck on their choice of words, did you say something that was perceived wrong? The identification of the failed communication brings an awareness for possible openness for change.

In rediscovering communication, it behooves us to think about what our values are, and how and why does one participate? We communicate for many different reasons, to feel a part of something or to be involved or to separate ourselves from the feelings that may be lurking deep inside. Communication between us and others brings about an effect within whether we are aware of it or not. At times, we are not aware of its impact and that it can affect us long after the conversation is finished. Have you ever noticed many hours or days can pass, and you think of what someone has said to you, and it sparks in you either delight or discomfort from the thought of it? Communication is just that powerful. It leaves a lasting trail.

I have found in my personal experiences when our intentions align with our authentic self we communicate from a perspective that is clear. This clarity sets everything else in motion to get our best-desired results. Communication is extremely necessary, and it is vital to be clear when we communicate to someone, as well as ourselves.

I have discovered there are five distinct types of dialogue that occur when we communicate. Let's take a closer look at each:

- Quality - A dialogue that has meaning to it and can be very motivational. It keeps interest, uplifts and intrigues all that are a part of it. This is the most recommended type of communication.

- Forced - A dialogue that you really don't want to be involved in, however, it makes its way into your space. It is forced upon you to respond or initiate dialogue. For example, you are walking down the street, and you see someone you know walking toward you. You cannot escape speaking, but you know the person is very chatty, and a simple hello from you will turn into a full blown conversation with this person.

- Choiceless - A dialogue that one encounters on a daily basis that may not have real value beyond the time of the incident. For example, purchasing gas, buying groceries and checking out at supermarket, etc.

- Unanticipated - A dialogue that is unexpected and causes an interruption. It is not necessarily unwanted, but it catches you by surprise. For example, while relaxing at your favorite coffee shop and someone enters and strikes up a conversation while you were having some alone time.

- One Way Communication - A dialogue where two or more people are involved, however, it appears that only one person is in the conversation with their self. For example, there is a group conversing where all members are expected to share and talk about their experiences, however, one member of the group has taken over the conversation and the other members feel as if they are being held hostage by the hijacker.

Exercise: *Think of a situation where you have experienced one of the five distinct types of dialogue. We find ourselves in one of them or all of them every day. Which one did you discover yourself in today?*

Since communication is part of our daily lives wouldn't we want the best out of it? Wouldn't you want to communicate to a level of influence that propels you to a state of comfort? A place where your natural state reflects itself. Quality dialogue is the Luminous Communication approach. Luminous - full of or shedding light, bright or shining, well lighted.

Usually, when communicating, we are only linked to what serves us and the feeling that's associated with it. We want immediate satisfaction from the dialogue. Choosing first to be clear on the five ways of communication will allow us to stay alert and warn us about the form we are using during a particular conversation. In this, we can make way for an elevated corresponding dialogue.

As we have heard, "NO MAN IS ISLAND." Human connectedness goes far beyond one's earthly comprehension and delves more into how to connect with others. On our island, communication must build gaps of understanding, it creates technology, new inventions, ceases loneliness temporarily, opens up possibilities, builds relationships and grows community.

Exercise: *Think of the most important value that communications serves a purpose for you. What does communication mean to you?*

Let's examine how we can transform dialogue with the use of Luminous Communication. Let's say we observe a conversation where one person is sharing, one is listening. With Luminous Communication, we want one of the parties to the conversation to stop and realize the point of the dialogue by identifying one of the five types of communication, to build on viewpoints identified and we want the end result to shed light upon a dynamic recognition of uplifting dialogue. Being unaware of the five types of communication, we don't know where the dialogue is going, there is no progress because it is quite possible that no one is being heard. A participant in the dialogue is most likely being left feeling unheard and unfulfilled and there seems to be no desired communication. With Luminous Communication, we can take a leap to realize the impact of the choice of words that we are using. This technique of examining the words that permeate our language and conversations is called Word Washing.

Word Washing allows us to redefine words and use brighter words that may have the same meaning, but it doesn't come with the same baggage to the listener. When we redefine a word, it gives us a clearer perspective on what is being said. It invites a refreshing nature from both parties involved in the dialogue. When the word comes across, we are left with an uplifted experience. This is Luminous Communication. Here are some examples of how Word Washing works. So let's revisit the conversation held between the two parties and instead of the talker using words in the first column

(Old language), she or he chooses to use the words in the second column (Luminous Communication). What do you think would be the desired outcome of the conversation?

Old language	Luminous Communication
Stuck	Refrained Movement
Problem	Concern
Wrong	Misdirected Choice
Stupid	Unconscious
Foolish	Unwise
Less	Decrease

Exercise: *Perhaps you can think of a word on your own and add a new spin to it.*

Let's go back way to the five distinct types of dialogue forms. Remember when engaged in any form of these dialogues, you have an opportunity to experience a luminous dialogue that will change the conversation to a much more vibrant dialogue with your involvement and the individual of which you encounter.

If we each participate in this technique of communicating, we will rise to a place of a magnetic connection and an overflowing sense of fullness that preserves, nurtures, radiates in a hearted temple of PEACE!

Having an experience with a word that illuminates your soul and serves you in a way that is fulfilling and inspiring makes for effective communication. Change the words that you are using that is causing miscommunication.

LUMINOUS COMMUNICATION constantly connects us to a higher level of interpersonal or intrapersonal relationships within ourselves and others, simultaneously while enhancing inspiration and motivation whether you have a brief encountering of one of the five distinct ways of communicating or a continuous conversation. I ask every individual to take part in this new way of communicating in some form or another. Take the first step of identifying and noticing where you fit in the five distinct types of communicating and then start using the Word Washing technique. Think what your purpose of communicating is for and adjust it to raise all. This will bring forth the best possible dialogue. Commit to sharing it with others. Think of a higher purpose where we all can converse in an engaging, balanced dialogue that will benefit and complement our place of being.

Luminous Communication Testimonials

This is what others have said about using Luminous Communication:

" A feeling of refreshed dialogue."

"Communication on the upswing."

"Never ending inspiration."

"A conversation that shines."

"Energizing."

"Complimentary interaction."

"Intriguing."

"Motivational and expansive."

"Sensational."

About Wanda Harris

Wanda Harris is a healer, teacher, and friend. She is a guided, gifted and intuitive individual who has spent the last two decades as a certified facilitator of the NAMELESS TECHNIQUE (a method of mental/physical releasing).

The NAMELESS TECHNIQUE is a unique approach for individuals who use verbal and written interactive exercises to aid in releasing behavioral patterns that cause mental and physical stresses.

The NAMELESS TECHNIQUE develops a heightened inner awareness that aligns one with personal growth goals. Her dynamism, humor, compassion, and love creates an uplifted and positive environment for her clients to grow and heal.

Wanda also lectures seminars and institutes ideas and programs targeted as "pioneers for a stress-free society."

Wanda Harris has an ongoing private practice in New Jersey.

To learn more about the NAMELESS TECHNIQUE or discovering your INNER BLUEPRINT,

Contact Wanda Today!

Website: http://stressfreesociety.net

Email: personalitymirroring@yahoo.com.

Chapter 21

5 Common Reasons Why Your Business Isn't Working (And How To Fix It)

Authored by Cindy Buccieri

Success means something different to each of us. Success can be linked to the amount of money you earn, the size of your home or the amount of stuff you have. But it's actually more about your mindset.

Science has shown a correlation between the brain, a person's positive attitude, and their body's response. Being positive can help an ailing body fight diseases better, and mentally to take on the challenges. Even if you fail or don't get the results you want it has been shown that it's easier to recover or continue on in a positive frame of mind.

It's your mindset that prevents you from being successful. It determines your patterns, behaviors and attitudes starting deep in the subconscious and then permeating your conscious state of being. Limiting negative thoughts, attitudes and behaviors set the tone, but if you identify them early and understand how they manifest in you and become part of your daily thoughts and behaviors, you can control them. If you don't pinpoint the sources of negativity, you cannot change them. It's that simple.

There are typically a few things that hold people back from achieving success. The good news is these can be changed.

Can't Get Out of Your Own Way

This means that for one reason or another you are sabotaging your success. Either you lack the confidence to believe that you deserve to have success, or you may believe that you know everything and aren't open to listening to other suggestions.

All of us are presented with other people's opinions of what we should be doing. It's up to us to listen to this advice and then decide if it's something that is in our best interest. The key is to be open.

Have you ever noticed that when you are faced with a question of how to do something you may hear something on the radio that spurs an idea or see an ad for a book that contains the answers you're looking for?

Many people have a hard time asking others for help. They confuse accepting help from others with weakness. This couldn't be farther from reality. Most successful people know about the importance of seeking and accepting help. They achieve their goals by leveraging other people's skills, strengths or contacts that they lack. At the same time, they offer their help to others and extend their circle of valuable relationships.

Additionally, resisting change can be associated with fear of the unknown. It is often evidenced by people who despite their unhappiness with their situation experience resistance to exploring opportunities for change. This resistance to change often leads to missed opportunities for advancement.

Don't Believe in Yourself

This one is the opposite of not being open to advice. This is the person who is unable to make a decision on their own. They ask tons of people for advice and then follow that advice to only be faced with disappointment. Why? Because it's not what is right for them.

All the answers we seek are within us. We just have to listen. I used to think meditation was reserved for monks. However, meditation has been extremely helpful in helping me find answers to my questions. Instead of letting others lead your life, try asking yourself for advice. You will also know when something is right for you by paying attention to your intuition or that "gut feeling." If it "feels" right, do it!

A healthy level of self-confidence and self-esteem is not only necessary, but it is also essential for any success we seek to achieve. Only when you're comfortable with who you are and confident in what you can do, will other people believe in you and your abilities. This applies both to your personal life as well as your professional life.

The other thing that keeps you in a state of being unable to change your mindset is the constant inner conversations you have with yourself. We all have these conversations both subconsciously and consciously. These thoughts feed our state of consciousness, as well. The first step to positivity is to change the negative conversations you have with yourself because they become your attitude. The way this can be done is through what is called the Three C's.

The Three C's are:

1. **Commitment** - Make a conscious commitment to be positive. This means committing yourself to positive things such as learning, family, friends, environment and positive causes. When you give others positive encouragement, it feeds your own positivity.

2. **Control** - Control your mind. Keep your mind focused on what is important in your life. You can foster this by setting goals and priorities for yourself and sticking to them. Learn to develop strategies to deal with problems. Be honest with yourself and learn to relax.

3. **Challenge** - Have courage in yourself and be courageous in your life. Do your best and don't look back. Seek learning and view change as opportunities, not setbacks. Consider your options if they fit your goals and dreams. Don't let anyone or anything prevent you from what you want. Try new things. Keep conscious track of your mental and physical health. Be

optimistic and do not surround yourself with negative people, things or situations.

Studies have shown people with the three C's are winners in good times and survivors in the bad. Research has also shown people who begin to modify and change their internal conversations with themselves find almost an immediate improvement in their performance and situation. It is commitment, control, and courage that helps a person become their best selves for themselves and then for the world.

Already Self-Defeated

Having a negative attitude is a sure-fire way to stifle success. Assuming that you won't close that sales deal, or you won't get that promotion, will more than likely result in that very outcome. This is right along with believing in yourself. If you think that things aren't going to work out for you, then what motivation do you have to move forward and pursue your dreams?

Passion is that driving force that propels us and gives us the courage to pursue those dreams. If people allowed their self-doubt to stop them, we wouldn't have some of the amazing inventions and companies that we have today. Believe and know that you are a powerful person who can achieve anything you put your mind to.

In essence, positivity is a mental attitude that is at the core of all our thoughts, words and actions, and enables our positive ideas to become reality. When we have a positive mindset, we can expect no less than a favorable outcome in our lives. When we live in a positive state, we can expect no less than health, joy and a good result in things we want in life. Truth be told, whatever the mind expects is what it finds. Don't be fooled, though, it takes work to be positive especially in a world such as ours today. But the more it is incorporated in our lives, the easier it becomes.

Don't Take Action

Nothing happens unless we take the steps in the right direction to make it happen. If you have a great idea for a business or product, nothing will happen by sitting on the couch. If you want to improve your health or improve your self-confidence, you have to take steps to eat better, exercise or learn how to love yourself.

Many people have great goals and visions. Unfortunately, the majority of people lose interest when the desired results don't materialize as quickly or easily as they anticipated; they give up and never try again. If you talk to people who have achieved great things in life, they will tell you that persistence is one of the key factors for their success. If you want to succeed, you need to be persistent.

I frequently meet people who want to start their own business. They have the dream but aren't yet taking the steps to achieve it. They have a million excuses as to why they haven't started.

If it's something you are passionate about you will find the time, and you will find the answers to the questions that are preventing you from moving forward.

Success is something that manifests in a person's life in different ways. Sometimes it may appear as a miracle and other times a subtle thing. It can be nothing more than an ordinary opportunity we have been waiting for that comes to being. Success may mean no more than a door opening, but it's up to you to see the door and go through it.

I encourage you to grab that brass ring that's in front of you. Your success is right there for the taking.

About Cindy Buccieri

Cindy Buccieri is the founder of the Inspired Living Community and Techie Girl Talks. She is also the author of Blogging the Right Way and CEO of CB Virtual Services. Her passion is helping others discover their purpose and live a happy and fulfilling life. Visit Cindy online at http://cindybuccieri.com for free resources and training tools to help you lead your best life and create a business you're passionate about. You Are Worth It!

Contact Cindy Today!

Websites:

http://cindybuccieri.com

http://inspiredlivingcommunity.com

http://techiegirltalks.com

Email: cindy@cindybuccieri.com

Facebook: http://facebook.com/cindybuccieripage

Twitter: http://twitter.com/cindybuccieri

Instagram: http://instagram.com/inspiredliving_cindy

Chapter 22

The Results Formula

Authored by Jean Oursler

Results have been my number one priority since I started my company. How do you measure results? How results-oriented are you? Do you always get the results that you want? Do you even know what results you would like to achieve? How you view results is often a barometer of how successful you are.

Not everyone is born results oriented; in fact, it is a learned skill. The good news is anyone and everyone can learn to be results oriented. One of my missions in life is to help others be more successful tomorrow than they are today. I have developed the

RESULTS Formula with you in mind. This formula is your master key to be more results oriented.

What is the RESULTS Formula? It is a seven-step process to follow that will improve your ability to get better results. In fact, I used the word RESULTS as an acronym to make it even easier to follow. HERE IT IS:

R: Ready

E: End

S: Steps

U: You

L: Levels

T: Transform

S: Success

Let's examine each letter in detail so that you can better understand what the RESULTS Formula means and how you can implement it so you can achieve greater outcomes.

R: READY

The "R" in the RESULTS formula stands for "Ready". Why ready? In order to achieve greater results, you need to be ready. Most people are not.

Ready means you have decided you want more, and you are willing to do what it takes to get it. It means you have realized that what you are doing is not working towards getting to the next level of success, and you realize it hasn't been working for some time.

Perhaps, you have been working for quite a while. You keep doing the same things over and over again. Each time you hope for a different or even better result. The problem is that is the definition of insanity: Doing the same thing over and over again hoping for a different result. Now you realize you have been practicing this insanity method and it is time to stop.

Let me give you an example. If I lined up ten people, six of them would be happy with what they are doing. They don't see the need to change or grow. They truly believe what they are doing right now is leading them to the success they have. Like it or not, I would call these people mediocre.

That leaves four people. Two of those are people who if they don't do something quickly they are going to fail. They are already on the slippery slope and are going downhill.

The other two are people I call "THE READY PEOPLE." The ready people are the ones who realize that they must improve every day in order to be more successful tomorrow. These are people who are ready. They are ready to meet whatever challenges are thrown their way. They are ready to change. They are ready to grow. They are ready for the next stage, and they want to be more successful. They know they must be more successful, or they will end up in the mediocre category or even worse, the slippery slope group.

My question to you is: ARE YOU READY? If so, read on.

E: END

The "E" in the RESULTS formula stands for "End". What do I mean by end? Once you are ready, you must think about what end results you want to achieve. What does the end result look like? The best way to achieve something is to visualize what outcome you want first.

By starting with the "end", you can then work backward to figure out the best way to begin. Most of my clients are not focused on the end results. They are focused on general outcomes. They know they need more sales, or they need to get the project completed by a certain deadline. However, often their outcomes are not results oriented. By thinking about the end and what you want to achieve, will make you think about the steps you need to obtain those results.

254

S: STEPS

Remember the ending outcome. Think about what you want to achieve, and then you will always think about the steps you need to obtain those results. The "S" in the RESULTS formula stands for "Steps". A helpful hint is thinking about the steps as action steps. The more specific you make these actions steps, the more likely to you achieve the results.

Here is a process to help you with your action steps. Write these action steps down. Put dates next to these action steps to ensure that they get done. Review these action steps either daily or weekly to keep them top of mind. These three steps will help you complete your action steps which will keep you on your path towards the results you desire.

U: YOU

The "U" in the RESULTS formula stands for "You". I know I have taken a bit of license in that the first letter in the word "you" is a "y". However, in this day and age, so many people use the letter "u" to stand for the word "you" that I thought I could use this substitute as well. Obviously in order to achieve greater results you need to be involved. During this time, you must also work on yourself and your abilities. You need to work on the specific skills that you need to achieve the results you desire. Once we graduate from school, many of us stop investing in ourselves. We stop learning. We don't pay the money to buy a book or go to a workshop or take a class or get a degree.

If you are seeking greater outcomes, then you must invest in yourself. Here are some suggestions to guide you. Find a coach. Find an accountability partner. Create a mastermind group. Do whatever it takes to improve yourself because as you improve your results will improve as well.

L: LEVELS

The "L" in the RESULTS formula stands for "Levels". What do I mean by levels? Because you are ready, you thought about the end result you want to achieve. You took the time to create and implement specific action steps, and you are focusing on improving yourself. As you acquire better skills, you are going to start going through different levels of learning.

You may feel uncomfortable at this time. You may feel frighten or frustrated because you are not sure this process is working. You may experience highs; you may experience lows. This is all part of the levels of learning. You are trying new ideas and improving different skills. You will fail, and you will be successful.

Levels of learning can be informal or formal. You can go back to school to get a higher degree, or you can read a book. You can attend a workshop or listen to an expert in your field. Levels of learning can happen anywhere and anytime as long as you are ready to receive the wisdom that is coming your way.

In this stage, the most important thing is that you are learning! I urge you to embrace the concept that you should never stop learning. Successful people never stop learning. Because successful people are always learning, they are always growing. You have to continue to grow to achieve. I can ensure you that your results will always be better if you are on a growth path than the person who is staying stagnant.

T: TRANSFORM

The "T" in the RESULTS formula stands for "Transform". When we go through levels of learning, we can't help but be transformed into a new way of thinking and a new way of being.

Transform means changing. I know there are so many people who are afraid of change. However, change is a part of life. I look at change and transformation as a great thing. Remember the time when there were no cell phones, iPads or even computers? How about electricity? All of these things transformed our lives, and we were happy to have them!

View change as positive. When you transform, you stop looking at the negative and only see the positive. You know you have transformed when you realize how you have changed from one point in time to another point in time.

S: SUCCESS

Transformation brings you to the last stage in the REULTS Formula. The "S" in the RESULTS Formula stands for "Success".

It takes hard work to achieve success. However, for almost all, achieving success is worth every step. When you get to success, celebrate. Most people don't. Why is it important to celebrate? Because our brains need a memorable reference point, also called a reward, to make the whole journey worthwhile!

Ways to celebrate include a dinner at your favorite restaurant, a piece of jewelry, a new watch or even a new car. There are lots of ways to reward yourself. You could reward yourself with a cruise or a pizza party. It doesn't matter if it is an experience or a tangible item. What matters is that your brain can recall the celebration and the success that went with it.

I worked with a management team for four years until the company sold. At the farewell party, the management team reviewed all their accomplishments along with every celebration. It wasn't a planned thing. They just started talking about the different events, the reasons why they were celebrating and the successes that went with them. Over the course of four years, they had 16 celebrations: one each quarter. They could remember each and every celebration in vivid detail. Can you remember what you did four years ago in vivid detail? How about last week?

That is why celebration is so important. It is an anchor that helps our brains remember the successes we have achieved. You can pre-plan your celebration or be spontaneous once you have achieved success. Either way, celebrate every success no matter how big or small because this reinforces why it is necessary to continue this lifelong RESULTS journey.

Conclusion

What is great about the RESULTS Formula is that it is repeatable. Once you achieve the RESULTS Formula, you can get yourself ready for the next level of success. When you are "ready" you can begin to implement the RESULTS Formula over and over again. You don't stop.

So many of us crave the next level of success, but few of us know how to achieve it. Now you have a proven formula that you can use to obtain the ultimate success you are seeking. Here is your proven formula. Go use it!

About Jean Oursler

Her clients have crowned Jean Oursler the Results Queen because they say she is all about getting the results they want. Jean specializes in Breakthrough Results with entrepreneurs, business owners, accountants, financial planners and lawyers who hate sales and marketing and want their business to grow and thrive.

Her clients make low six-figure new business development sales within the first 12 months or less doing it in a way that makes them feel comfortable.

Are you ready to achieve the Breakthrough RESULTS!?

Contact Jean today!

Websites:

For entrepreneurs: http://www.womengetresults.com

For financial services: http://www.practicemanagement.com

Email: jean@moreresultsnow.com

Final Thoughts

"Breakthrough Results" just don't happen. You have to make them happen. This is true whether it is in your personal life or your business life. The authors in this book have given you great tips, tricks, and techniques that can help you achieve the amazing results that you want and deserve, however, I know you are facing challenges. How do I know that? I know because my clients are facing the same challenges. The authors have told me their clients are facing these challenges. What are they?

One challenge you may be facing is you need to get started and you can't, so you stopped. Another challenge is you have tried something from this book, and it didn't work the way you expected, so you stopped. Here is another, picking something to work on from this book and then you get distracted or worse, stuck, and you stopped. There seems to be a theme.

The theme is that you stopped. When you are working towards achieving "Breakthrough Results," you can't stop. Think about climbing Mount Everest. There are people who want to and never get started, so they stop. There are those who try, and it didn't work out the way the wanted to, so they stopped. There are those that start and get distracted or worse, stuck. That is when disaster happens. It is only those climbers who don't stop and know when to ask for help who summit the mountain. These climbers truly achieve "Breakthrough Results." How are you summiting your "Breakthrough Results" mountain?

The authors in this book are here to help you. So when you stop, I would urge you to reach out to that specific author and get their help. Go to their website, send them an email, or simply call them. Do not accept being stopped. Once you do, you will not achieve the "Breakthrough Results" you want. We are all here to help you, so don't be a stranger. We all look forward to helping you with your "Breakthrough Results" journey.

Jean Oursler

The Results Queen™

www.ingramcontent.com/pod-product-compliance
Lightning Source LLC
Chambersburg PA
CBHW060335200326
41519CB00011BA/1947